ENOUGH
BULL

ENOUGH BULL

HOW TO RETIRE WELL WITHOUT THE STOCK MARKET, MUTUAL FUNDS OR EVEN AN INVESTMENT ADVISOR

David Trahair, CA

**Author of the National Bestseller *Smoke and Mirrors:
Financial Myths That Will Ruin Your Retirement Dreams***

WILEY

John Wiley & Sons Canada, Ltd.

Library and Archives Canada Cataloguing in Publication
Trahair, David
   Enough bull : how to retire well without the stock market, mutual funds, or even an investment advisor / David Trahair.

ISBN 978-0-470-16127-2

   1. Retirement income—Planning. 2. Finance, Personal. I. Title.

HG179.T72 2009   332.024'014   C2009-902565-5

Production Credits
Cover Design: Ian Koo
Interior Design: Adrian So
Typesetter: Thomson Digital
Printer: Friesens

Editorial Credits
Executive Editor: Karen Milner
Project Coordinator: Pauline Ricablanca

John Wiley & Sons Canada, Ltd.
6045 Freemont Blvd. .
Mississauga, Ontario
L5R 4J3

Printed in Canada

1 2 3 4 5 FP 13 12 11 10 09

ENVIRONMENTAL BENEFITS STATEMENT

John Wiley saved the following resources by printing the pages of this book on chlorine free paper made with 100% post-consumer waste.

TREES	WATER	SOLID WASTE	GREENHOUSE GASES
71	32,663	1,983	6,782
FULLY GROWN	GALLONS	POUNDS	POUNDS

Calculations based on research by Environmental Defense and the Paper Task Force.
Manufactured at Friesens Corporation

TABLE OF CONTENTS

ACKNOWLEDGEMENTS

I'd like to start off by thanking the two people that are responsible for the creation of this book. Those people are my literary agent, Hilary McMahon of Westwood Creative Artists, and Karen Milner of John Wiley & Sons Canada, Ltd., my publisher. If not for Hilary's belief in the idea and Karen's enthusiasm for seeing it get into print, you wouldn't be holding it right now.

I'd like to dedicate it to two other significant people in my life. First, to my mom, Florence Trahair, who passed away in 2008 at age eighty-two. She was always my biggest supporter. I felt her presence as I wrote this book. And second, to my father-in-law, Jack Baxter, who passed away in 2006 at age sixty-eight. Jack was one of my best buddies. He taught me how to enjoy life. I know he enjoyed each and every day of his.

INTRODUCTION

We have just lived through a period of time that shifted the financial world on its axis. The old rules regarding personal finance are now history, as in obsolete.

This happened in the last quarter, the autumn, of 2008. Let's call it "The Fall of 2008."

THE FALL OF 2008

During this period, decades-old financial institutions simply disappeared. World stock markets tanked. Entire investment portfolios were devastated. Retirement dreams were wiped out. And it's probably not going to get better soon.

What this series of events has done is show quite clearly the naked truth: traditional financial planning techniques don't work. In fact, if we had done the opposite of what the "experts" have told us to do to get ahead financially, we would be far better off today. Here are some of the past theories and the new reality:

- Trust the stock market to make us wealthy? Never again.
- Pay our investment advisor a fee of more than 2% a year to try to beat the market? I don't think so.
- Risk our home trying to "make our mortgage tax deductible" by investing in mutual funds? Please, give me a break.

- Maximize our RRSP contributions religiously each and every year . . . and also save 10% of our income above that. You must be kidding, right?
- Borrow to invest—"leverage" our way to riches? Forget it. Many have tried; you can now find most of them in the poorhouse.
- Skip a cup of coffee to get rich automatically? Yeah, right.

I am not opposed to capitalism. We need efficient stock markets so that entrepreneurial people can grow businesses that flourish—businesses that create great products, deliver excellent services, hire good people, make profits and pay taxes.

The problem is that, obviously, markets have not been regulated satisfactorily. Businesses, especially financial ones in the United States, have been allowed to run rampant in the quest for riches. Thousands of intelligent, well-educated people making six-figure salaries and multi-million dollar bonuses spent years creating complex financial products that were sold to unsuspecting members of the public.

Ever heard of collateralized debt obligations? Mortgage-backed securities? Non-bank asset-backed commercial paper? What about income trusts? Or even mutual funds?

These complex instruments made many people rich. The people that invented them. The people that re-packaged them. And the people that sold them.

Unfortunately, the vast majority of people that bought into them got screwed. There's the homeowner with no job and no money who was convinced to take out a mortgage on his home and ended up losing it. There's the government, and you and me as the taxpayers, forced to shell out billions of dollars to buy into financial houses-of-cards just to keep them afloat. And of course, there's anyone who holds investments in these worthless companies.

ANGRY YET?

I am, and that's why I wrote this book. To give you hope. To show you that there is a way to get ahead financially. And you don't have to be a genius or trust a financial expert to get you there.

I'm going to show you how you can do it with a guarantee that in the future your investments will never decline. I can say that because we won't be using the stock market. We won't even be using mutual funds. It is so easy to follow you won't even need to think about it for more than a few hours a year. It is so simple that once implemented you won't even need an investment advisor.

It's the plan laid out in this book that you can read in less than one day. After you read this book you'll be able to explain it fully in five minutes.

WHY I WROTE THIS BOOK

I wrote it because I have received a lot of e-mails like this:

> *Good morning, David. I have just finished reading your book* Smoke and Mirrors: Financial Myths That Will Ruin Your Retirement Dreams *and I couldn't agree with you more. I am, however, concerned about my daughter and son-in-law who have this mantra that everything goes into the RRSP. I need to educate them and your line of thinking is what I need to approach them with.*
>
> *While my children are quite well off, I am scraping by—having lost most of my portfolio in the recent stock market crash while my husband was going through a major cancer operation and my portfolio was not on my mind and, sad to say, nor on my broker's mind. The good thing is hubby survived, but our belts are very tight as a result of looking the other way for even a few days.*
>
> *Joanne*

This e-mail arrived in January of 2005. The stock market crash she was talking about was the crash of March of 2000. In 2008 I started to hear more such stories.

YOUR RETIREMENT JOURNEY

But does the whole idea of financial planning need to be so complex? If you listen to all the experts, you'll often end up confused. You may be thinking:

- My investment advisor is telling me I have to invest more but my existing savings have just gotten whacked in the market. Isn't that like throwing good money after bad?
- Getting my finances in order is going to be painful. Forget it. I want to live now!
- This is all so depressing. I never seem to be making much progress.
- All the standard retirement advice says that I'm on the wrong track. Jeez, my unused RRSP room is huge!
- Personal finances are very complex; I can never get a good handle on what is going on with my money even after talking to my broker.
- I may never be able to afford to retire!

You know what? It doesn't have to be confusing or complicated. It never used to be. Things like mutual funds, RRSPs and even capital gains tax did not even exist before the seventies. The truth is that the whole subject of personal finance has been made complicated because it makes money for the people that run the financial system. It is designed to be complex so that these financial types can continue to earn six-figure salaries—off the hard-earned savings of the little guy and gal.

Let's make an analogy, shall we? They want us to believe that the typical journey to retirement is like a trip down a river. A river is the best way to get there—walking is too slow. It's a complicated journey, so you'll obviously need a guide, right?

Down the River

We arrive at our advisor's headquarters to learn about the trip we are about to take.

"Welcome friends, you've come to the right place! We have been in business for more than twenty years and we know rivers like the back of our hands. Trust us—we'll get you to your destination safely."

The advisor goes on to describe the trip.

"Rivers are different and you never really know what to expect. We have accompanied our clients on thousands of river trips. We know what to expect! We know how to guide you through rough waters. Don't worry—let our experience be your guide!"

"Now step into the next office, where we'll teach you all about what you're likely to see and experience during the journey."

So you step through the door and are asked to sign the "Know Your Client" form. This form is necessary for the advisor. It proves you OK'd some level of risk taking. If you read the fine print, you'll see that the onus is on you to protect yourself.

Now, in this case, the advisor doesn't know which river you're going to be travelling down. If he has had little experience, he may have only travelled down easy flowing rivers with nice scenery.

The more experienced advisors know that most trips are never soothing for long. They know the trip may be anything but.

If they were forced into full disclosure, they'd have to warn you of the truth:

Most retirement journeys using the stock market are like a journey down the river—the Niagara River!

Uh-Oh, It's the Niagara River

Here's what you should know before you begin the journey. According to Niagara Parks, an agency of the Government of Ontario, the Niagara River is 58 kilometres long, beginning in Lake Erie and ending in Lake Ontario. The elevation between the lakes is about 99 metres (326 feet). About half of that elevation change occurs at one spot—Niagara Falls.

At Grand Island, the river divides into the west channel, known as the Canadian or Chippawa Channel, and the east channel, known as the American or Tonawanda Channel.

The Canadian Horseshoe Falls drops an average of 57 metres (188 feet) while the American Falls ranges from 21 to 34 metres (70 to 110 feet). The American measurement is taken from the top of the falls to the top of the rock pile at the base, called the Talus Slope. The height of the American Falls from the top of the falls to the river below the rocks is the same as the Canadian Horseshoe Falls.

Sections of the river move quite slowly, but the speed of the water in the rapids just above the falls reaches 40 kilometres per hour

(25 miles per hour). Speeds of over 100 kilometres per hour (60 miles per hour) have been recorded at the falls themselves. At the Whirlpool Rapids below the falls, water travels at about 50 kilometres per hour (30 miles per hour).

The great volume of water going over the falls is forced into a narrow gorge called the Great Gorge, where the Whirlpool Rapids are formed. The water surface here drops 15 metres (50 feet) and the water speeds reach 9 metres per second (30 feet per second). The whirlpool is a basin formed where the river takes a sharp right turn. The actual whirlpool is created by the "reversal phenomenon." Here, the water travels over the rapids and enters the pool, then travels counterclockwise past the natural outlet. When the exiting water tries to cut across itself to reach the outlet, pressure builds up and forces the water under the incoming stream. The swirling waters create a vortex or whirlpool.

Beyond the whirlpool is another set of rapids that drops approximately 12 metres (40 feet).

"Are you ready?" your advisor then asks. "Let's jump into the boat then, shall we?"

Assume your journey to retirement is the 58-kilometre stretch from Lake Erie to Lake Ontario along the Niagara River. It would be an exciting trip, wouldn't it? Some parts would be calm and slow, others bumpy and very fast. There would be smooth sections and jaw-dropping plunges. There would be parts where you'd feel like you were going nowhere— spinning in circles. There'd possibly even be some rocky sections. Doesn't that sound a lot like the typical trip to retirement using the stock market?

Retirement Journey: Plan B

But is a trip down Niagara the only way to get to Lake Ontario? In personal finance terms, is trusting the stock market to carry our retirement nest egg to our destination the best way to go?

I don't think so. Personally, I'd rather avoid the jaw-dropping plunges. Decisions like whether to go over the Canadian Falls, or the smaller American Falls with the rock slope at the bottom, are decisions I don't care to make!

I also don't like the idea of spinning around a whirlpool at a hundred kilometres an hour hoping I don't drown. And I'd prefer a smooth ride to one that might throw me out of the boat.

Here's What They Don't Want You to Know

Well, here's what they don't want you to know: you don't need to use the Niagara River. You don't need the stock market or mutual funds. You don't need to risk your financial life by going over spectacular plunges or stagnating for endless periods of time going around in circles hoping you won't drown in the process.

You can take the guaranteed route—the safe road—and this book will show you how.

PART ONE: THE ANTIDOTE

THE ANTIDOTE: A SIX-POINT PLAN FOR FINANCIAL FREEDOM

The Antidote is a simple plan. It'll only take you a few minutes to read the six-point synopsis below.

But here is the best thing about it: You don't need to follow it in order. You don't even need to religiously follow each one of the six points. The fact of the matter is that even if you stick to just one of the points, you'll probably make a significant improvement in your personal finances.

Follow it and you can rest easy knowing that your retirement nest egg will never decline, even if your bank does.

Here we go.

1. Avoid Personal Financial Disasters

- Never touch anything that cannot be explained simply to you in plain English.
- Don't invest in anything that is not guaranteed by the government.
- Never borrow to invest.
- Avoid complicated investment schemes. If it sounds too good to be true, it is.

2. You Don't Need the Stock Market or Mutual Funds

- The truth is that you don't need to risk your hard-earned money in the stock market and you don't need mutual funds.
- You can use 100% government-guaranteed investment certificates to achieve your goals without the risk of losing your shirt.
- If you want to take a chance, buy a lottery ticket.

3. Buy a Home and Pay Off the Mortgage

- Decide if you can afford a house and, if you can, buy one.
- Do the calculation of how many years it will take to pay off the mortgage and do it.
- Never risk your home for any kind of investment idea, no matter what.

4. Reducing Expenses Doesn't Have to Be Painful

- Focus on two of your biggest expenses—income taxes and interest on your debt.
- Pay to have your family's personal income tax returns prepared by a qualified expert.
- Pay extra to have that expert analyze your family situation to maximize savings by income splitting, restructuring to make sure as much debt as possible is tax-deductible.
- Find out what your credit rating is and improve it.
- Get at least three quotes on any debt that you get into.

5. Forget RRSPs Until Your Debt Is Paid Off (the Opportunity Zone)

- Do not even think about saving for retirement until you have paid off student loans and bought a home.
- Pay off your mortgage before investing another dime in an RRSP.
- Never borrow to invest in an RRSP.

6. Ask Yourself if You Really Need an Investment Advisor

- If you've got a bad one, find a good one.
- If you can't find a good one, simplify your finances so you don't need one at all.

1

AVOID PERSONAL
FINANCIAL DISASTERS

In the mid-eighties I took one of those personality tests that determine what type of person you are, what your strengths and weaknesses are and what type of career you'd be suited for. The results were not too surprising: I was basically a pretty normal person, good at math, probably never going to be a great artist or preacher.

But then, at the end of the session, the person giving me the results told me something that has turned out to be one of the most important pieces of information that I have ever received in my life. It was this:

Dave, you can't tell when people are lying to you.

What? You mean I can't tell by looking directly into someone's eyes and monitoring their body language whether they are telling me the truth? Exactly.

And you know what? Neither can you.

Think about it. Ever watched a great actor in a movie? There are great actors all around us each and every day. The problem is that some of them want to rip us off.

I was fortunate enough to learn this lesson in my twenties and it has stood me in good stead when it comes to investing, as well as life in general. I don't assume everyone I meet is lying to me. For example, I have known my buddy Stu for more than thirty years and I know I can trust him because he has never once lied to me.

On the other hand, I initially do not trust people I meet for the first time, even if they have been referred by a friend or client.

Unfortunately, many people did not take the personality test in their twenties that I did. They learned the hard way that many people can't be trusted. One of the early examples when it comes to investing rip-offs was that of Charles Ponzi.

THE PONZI SCHEME

This scheme is often referred to when it comes to schemes that have ripped off investors.

Charles Ponzi (pronounced "pon-zee") was born in Italy in 1882 as Carlo Ponzi. He grew up there and emigrated to the U.S. in 1903 at the age of twenty-one.

His first stop? Canada. He went to Montreal, where he was convicted of forgery in 1908 and sentenced to three years in prison. After his early release for good behaviour he was soon arrested on immigration charges for trying to assist five other people get into the U.S. illegally. He was jailed again in 1910.

After his release, he spent time in various cities and held various jobs, including dishwasher, waiter and office clerk. He eventually settled down in Boston in 1917, where he worked in clerical office jobs.

On December 26, 1919, Ponzi established a company called the Securities Exchange Company. He had hit upon an idea to make himself rich. It had to do with postal international reply coupons (IRCs). These were coupons that could be exchanged for one or more postage stamps for the minimum postage for an airmail letter to be returned to any other country that was a member of the Universal Postal Union. The purpose of an IRC is to send someone a letter in another country with sufficient postage for them to send a reply. For letters in the same country you can simply use a self-addressed stamped envelope, but for mailings to other countries, using an IRC does away with the need to use foreign postage or currency.

Ponzi claimed that he could make money by taking advantage of different postal and exchange rates in different countries. For example, he claimed he could send $1 to Italy and with the IRC he could buy $3.30 worth of stamps in Boston. He promised up to a 50% return in ninety days. In the beginning he actually did pay that rate of return—often in only forty-five days.

To many people, it sounded like a good idea. The money started to flow in.

Within a few months people began lining up at his company's door. Thousands of people invested their hard-earned savings. At its peak the company was bringing in more than $1 million a week, and that was in the early 1920s.

The problem was that he never really bought the IRCs or even attempted to make any money for the investors. He simply paid the return out of the money that previous investors had put in. Prior to Ponzi this was simply known as "robbing Peter to pay Paul."

It was so devastating that even the U.S. Securities and Exchange Commission (SEC) devotes a page to it.

Here's what it says:

Ponzi schemes are a type of illegal pyramid scheme named for Charles Ponzi, who duped thousands of New England residents into investing in a postage stamp speculation scheme back in the 1920s. Ponzi thought he could take advantage of differences between U.S. and foreign currencies used to buy and sell international mail coupons. Ponzi told investors that he could provide a 40% return in just 90 days compared with 5% for bank savings accounts. Ponzi was deluged with funds from investors, taking in $1 million during one three-hour period—and this was 1921! Though a few early investors were paid off to make the scheme look legitimate, an investigation found that Ponzi had only purchased about $30 worth of the international mail coupons.

Decades later, the Ponzi scheme continues to work on the "rob-Peter-to-pay-Paul" principle, as money from new investors is

*used to pay off earlier investors until the whole scheme col-
lapses. (U.S. Securities and Exchange Commission, "Ponzi"
schemes. http://www.sec.gov/answers/ponzi.htm.)*

How could people fall for a scheme that promised such huge returns in so little time? Well, they did, and they continue to do so.

If you look up Charles Ponzi in Wikipedia, under "Similar Schemes"
you'll see a new name: Bernard Madoff—Bernie to his friends.

Bernie Madoff

Bernard L. Madoff was arrested on December 11, 2008, by U.S. federal authorities in New York City on charges that he perpetrated a
massive securities fraud on the investors in his investment advisory
business. Estimates of the losses range between US$17 billion and
US$50 billion.

A *New York Times* article dated December 11, 2008, (http://www.
nytimes.com/2008/12/12/business/12scheme.html) quotes an associate director of enforcement for the U.S. SEC as calling it "a stunning
fraud that appears to be of epic proportions." If the figures reveal themselves to be true, it could be the largest fraud ever committed on Wall
Street.

According to recent federal filings, Bernard L. Madoff Investment
Securities, the firm Madoff started in 1960, held $17 billion in more
than two dozen funds.

The funds had been widely marketed to wealthy investors, hedge
funds and other large institutional investors for decades. The Madoff
funds promised high returns with low fees.

It seems that part of the reason that this scheme lasted so long was
that the returns promised and reported seem to be high but not out-
rageously so. For example, one of Madoff's funds, the Fairfield Sentry
Limited Fund, reported assets of US$7.3 billion in October 2008 and
claimed to have paid more than 11% interest each year during its
fifteen-year track record, according to the *Times* article.

I guess Bernie learned his lessons from Charles Ponzi well.

How did he do this? How did he convince dozens of sophisticated
investors and financial institutions to trust him with their funds?

Well, one of the reasons is that he appeared to be a nice guy, with little or no ego. He used to tell interviewers that he got his initial earnings to start his firm in 1960 by working as a lifeguard at city beaches and installing underground sprinkler systems.

In fact, I just watched a thirty-four-minute video of Madoff that was posted on YouTube.com, entitled "Bernie Madoff on the modern stock market." It was a roundtable discussion on October 20, 2007, shortly after the subprime mortgage crisis started in the U.S. with stock markets riding high. One of his employees, a computer programming expert, sits beside him throughout.

During the video, he exudes charm. He says he employs highly educated MBAs, but he himself was "happy to graduate college." At one point he hired engineers from MIT to help with the computer trading models the firm employs but they "think too much." That gets a laugh from the audience.

He seems to know what he is talking about. He seems to be an expert. He never interrupts anyone. He'd be the kind of guy you'd want to introduce your kids to if they wanted to get into the investment industry. Well, except for the fact that you now know that he is a consummate con artist.

A couple of the most interesting comments actually come at the end from the audience. One individual in the investment industry makes the point that most people who invest big money in the stock market actually made their fortune somewhere else—in an actual business—and bring the money to the market in an attempt to make more. They did not become wealthy by buying stocks!

Madoff's employee, a guy who at the time made his living investing, makes the point that the market is fuelled by greed and fear. He goes on to talk about greed being a slow process, and fear happening fast. When markets are going up month by month, year by year, people get in. Some start early, some late. Some invest a lot, some not so much. When things go bad, the "herd mentality" causes people to panic. The fear of losing money causes everyone to act. They all sell. Markets crash, and they crash quickly.

Yeah, we know.

I realize that Bernie Madoff is an American dealing with large wealthy investors, so you may not be able to relate to the plight of the people who trusted him. But, con artists don't just exist in New York. They live everywhere, even in Canada.

OUR VERY OWN CANADIAN FRAUD

The Eron Mortgage fraud happened in British Columbia. That is not a typo. It's not the "Enron" fraud. It's our own very Canadian fraud.

What's different about this fraud is that a detailed study of the ins and outs of how and why it happened was performed. And the results are intriguing.

The report is titled "Eron Mortgage Study." The principal researcher was Neil Boyd, LL.B., LL.M., Professor and Associate Director, School of Criminology at Simon Fraser University. The full study is available for download from Boyd's website at http://www.neilboyd.net/.

The study, conducted in 2004 and 2005, is the first comprehensive study of an investment fraud and includes responses from more than 2,200 Eron Mortgage investors. This was a detailed project. Researchers reviewed relevant existing research on investment fraud; reviewed the B.C. Securities Commission findings on the case; held several focus groups; and distributed two sets of surveys—an initial one to 520 random Eron investors and a refined, final version to 1,765 investors. They also conducted 180 telephone interviews and had face-to-face meetings with regulators, legal counsel, accountants and other experts in securities legislation and investor fraud.

The first thing that strikes you is the sheer number of victims. Roughly 2,800 people became prey to this one scheme and this is just one private market deal in one Canadian province.

The second thing that hits you is the absolutely devastating effect that losing money in this scam had on people. Consider this quote received from an Eron investor:

It made sense to me. Joe Blow has a piece of property but can't proceed, because of not having capital to proceed. Therefore he borrows money at high interest until he gets the infrastructure together for this project that he's hoping to have happen. As soon as he's got something, the banks or someone else can mortgage it for him, and he would pay back the high interest loan.

A friend of a friend that told me about Eron, and at the time I was a struggling single parent, and he encouraged me and an awful lot of others to invest in this . . . so I invested all the savings I had—about $14,000. All I remember is that I was a single parent and was struggling. I know that to some people the $14,000 wasn't much, but it was disastrous to me.

That's often the "hook": the ideas seem to make some logical sense. The other thing to take careful note of is the personal connection angle. Boyd's research on the dynamics of victimization indicated that frauds are most likely to be successful if the victim has some kind of personal tie to the con artist. In most cases, the initial contact was in person or through a third party, television or the media as opposed to mail or telephone.

What Did the "Average" Victim Look Like?

There was no common attribute among survey respondents, no single "flaw" that researchers could find. Most (61%) of the investors were male and working at the time of the investment. The average age of the Eron investors was fifty-five at the time of first investment, with approximately 64% over age forty-five at that time.

They seemed to be no better educated or more affluent than the average British Columbian of similar age. About one-third had a University education, one-third had some college or post-secondary training and the rest were either high school graduates or did not complete secondary education.

The majority also were not wealthy. At the time, about two-thirds had total annual household incomes of less than $75,000, with only 12% reporting that it was over $100,000. This is similar to the average Canadian.

The majority (60%) had a household net worth of under $250,000 excluding their principal residence.

Almost half (48%) considered themselves conservative investors and fully 78% admitted they were not "very knowledgeable of the securities market and mortgage investments."

The study seems to confirm the desire to attain wealth the "easy" way. While 62% thought the Eron investment was no-risk or low-risk, the number one reason people were attracted was the high guaranteed rate of return. Sophisticated investors would know there is no such thing as a high guaranteed rate of return. In this case, 34% of the investors did not even know they were investing—they thought they were providing a loan with a guaranteed rate of return.

How Did Investors Become Involved in Eron?

Most of them heard about Eron through family and friends; however, Eron seminars, brokers, and newspaper and television ads were also important. Most respondents (55%) read the Eron investor prospectus, but it is not clear that that would have done any good as there is no proof it was an honest document. Since this was not a public company, it did not have to file a prospectus with the B.C. Securities Commission.

What Steps Did Investors Take Before Investing?

Less than half the investors took additional steps beyond reading the prospectus. These steps included viewing photographs of the project, consulting with family and friends who were involved, speaking with other investors or visiting the Eron offices. It is not clear, though, if this would have done any good in this case, as it was a bogus operation.

Very few people took steps that may have warned them early enough. Only 13% reviewed audited financial statements, 11% sought independent professional advice, 7% actually visited the properties and 6% checked with regulatory agencies.

Only 2% of the investors bothered to check the backgrounds of the two principals that invented the scheme. If they had, they would have found out that both had been bankrupt before and had a history of failed businesses. This may have been enough to discourage some, but a background check is not a fail-safe way to protect yourself. Remember, Bernie Madoff was the chairman of the NASDAQ stock exchange at one point and had a very good reputation.

Why Did They Invest?

When asked the main purpose of their Eron investment, 58% said to build their retirement savings. The next most common answer, at 19% was to enhance current lifestyle. This is a significant finding. It means that many people are worried about financing their retirement and are willing to take significant risk to try to solve the problem.

This makes many people pre-disposed to being ripped off. Retiring well involves a bit of work and those who say you can simply hand your money over and walk away knowing you're being well taken care of are probably trying to make money off you.

Where Did They Get the Money?

Tragically, in most cases the money used for investing in the scheme was not from excess savings but from existing retirement savings, mortgages on their homes and loans from financial institutions. Boyd's conclusion is that "a significant number of the investors jeopardized their financial security because of their apparent concerns for their financial futures."

In other words, in pursuit of their goals they ignored point number one of a successful retirement strategy: avoid situations that could lead to personal financial disaster.

The Lessons of Eron

The lessons of Eron are simple:

- **Don't believe anyone that says they can guarantee a high rate of return.** Achieving a high rate of return means accepting risk—the risk that you could lose it all.
- **Knowing someone involved does not help.** In fact, it often does more harm than good. People seem to "let their guard down" when friends or family are involved.

- **Investment education is the best defence.** Trying to blame securities regulators after the loss is essentially a waste of time. Educate and protect yourself—don't get involved in the first place.
- **Check the background of the people involved.** In this case both principals had gone bankrupt before. Would you trust your life savings with them?

EXTRAORDINARY POPULAR DELUSIONS

Beware that disaster can strike even if there is no con artist. People's own lust for wealth can lead to disaster all by itself. All you have to do is think back to the dot-com bubble around the year 2000. People were freely investing in companies that did not have any profits. In fact, many companies did not even have any *revenues*. All they had were ideas. Buying pet food over the Internet, anyone?

This is not a new concept. Recently I read a great book called *Extraordinary Popular Delusions and the Madness of Crowds* (Charles Mackay, 1980) that details sixteen different cases of people losing their heads, and then their shirts, over the latest "sure thing."

It includes the tale of Tulipomania, where more than a few lost fortunes on a single tulip bulb! (The story of the merchant who ate a tulip mistaking it for an onion is worth the price of the book.)

It also includes the story of the South-Sea Bubble of England in the 1700s, where thousands were left penniless believing the South-Sea Company would make them rich through free trade with the ports of South America. During this period it seemed everyone wanted to invest in almost any idea imaginable to get rich.

One such company's prospectus actually stated its purpose as: "For carrying on an undertaking of great advantage; but nobody to know what it is." The government had to declare it illegal just to prevent people from investing in it!

But probably the most important lesson of the book is what happened after the South-Sea bubble scam had been exposed. Everyone was after the heads of the directors of the South-Sea Company, who by their fraudulent practices had brought the nation to virtual ruin. Here's what Mackay says:

Nobody seemed to imagine that the nation itself was as culpable as the South-Sea Company. Nobody blamed the credulity and avarice of the people—the degrading lust for gain, which had swallowed up every nobler quality in the national character, or the infatuation which had made the multitude run their heads with such frantic eagerness into the net held out for them by scheming projectors. These things were never mentioned. The people were a simple, honest, hard-working people, ruined by a gang of robbers, who were to be hanged, drawn and quartered without mercy.
(Charles Mackay, *Extraordinary Popular Delusions and the Madness of Crowds* [New York: Harmony Books, 1980], 72)

This is an important point that was also made in the Eron Mortgage Study. Sure, there are con artists and there always will be. But the con artists cannot be successful if people don't fall for their schemes.

OTHER POTENTIAL DISASTERS

It's not just chasing the riches promised by schemers that can lead to financial ruin. There are many other possible disasters awaiting Canadians. Here are but a few:

Credit Card Disease

I once had an e-mail from a gentleman whose credit card debt exceeded his family's total gross salary. He said they simply could not afford to live without credit cards. While most Canadians aren't in this bad a situation, a large percentage—the card companies say it's approximately 50%—carry a balance month to month. In other words, they spend more than they make, using credit cards to make that possible.

This is not only a waste of money (with interest charges at 20% or more), it can lead to the ultimate personal financial disaster: bankruptcy. But you know what? This is not the credit card companies' fault. And while you could argue that the rates are excessively high, the companies are not forcing consumers to use their cards. The problem is the spending habits of the people.

That's why it's so hard to pay off a credit card balance. You may be able to pay a big chunk down but the additional charges during the last month often offset any paydown. Add the fuel of easy credit card availability and many Canadians are putting their whole financial future at risk.

Taking Out a Mortgage on Your Home to Invest

You could end up losing your investment . . . and your house.

The Latest Stock Chase

Many people seem to want to get rich, easily and quickly. What better way than the latest stock market darling? Enron, WorldCom, Nortel, Bre-X anyone? Look at what just happened in China—many hard-working people lost more than 50% of their "blood and sweat money" in a matter of months. The folly of this strategy usually becomes clear too late.

Trusting Your "Friends"

There are more and more stories surfacing these days about out-and-out fraud by "investment advisors." Now obviously, I don't want to paint all advisors with the same brush, but many people place their retirement in the hands of friends or even relatives that are simply unqualified or are even rip-off artists.

Mortgage Fraud

Imagine a senior having paid off the home mortgage, only to have it stolen from her by an unscrupulous thief.

HOW TO PREVENT PERSONAL FINANCIAL DISASTERS

You need to have preventative controls in place so you don't get conned. In other words, don't expect a "big brother" to bail you out of a stupid decision. In most cases the government, the securities regulators and other watchdogs are not even responsible for trying to recover your money.

Avoid getting sucked in altogether. As Boyd states in his report's conclusion to the Eron Mortgage fraud:

We can make improvements to regulatory law so that it better protects investors, but it will ultimately be a well-informed and skeptical investor who is less likely to be victimized by the fraudulent dishonesty of men like Brian Slobogian and Frank Biller. (Neil Boyd, Eron Mortgage Study: Final Report [March 31, 2005], 37)

CONCLUSION

Very few people think about this, but avoiding personal financial disasters should be the number one rule of personal finance. Unfortunately, the vast majority of Canadians make at least one major mistake in their personal finances during their life. This often puts them back years and can result in financial devastation.

And just how do they get into these disastrous situations? By falling for the slick sales pitches of unqualified advisors and in some cases outright con artists. The best way to avoid the disasters is to avoid the schemes that can lead to them.

If you take just one thing from this book, make it this one.

YOU DON'T NEED THE STOCK MARKET OR MUTUAL FUNDS

THE WORLDWIDE ECONOMIC MELTDOWN

I first started to write this chapter on Monday, October 6, 2008. By noon on that day the S&P/TSX Composite Index had dropped more than 1,000 points since the market opened in the morning. That is a decline of over 11% in a few hours. By the end of the day the decline had been reduced to 572 points. They say the stock market is volatile, but this is ridiculous. What's worse is that this day had come after already jaw-dropping declines since the index peaked in June of 2008.

Let's dig a little deeper into what has just happened in Canada from June to the end of November 2008, because this is a period of time that people will be talking about for generations to come.

Check out the following chart that shows the weekly closing values of the S&P/TSX Composite Index from the highest peak it has reached—June 18, 2008—to November 17, 2008.

In that five-month period, more than 45% of the value of the index was lost. In one week alone at the beginning of October, more than 16% was lost.

That's when I started receiving phone calls from friends asking for advice. What would you tell a single mother who has just lost half of

S&P/TSX Composite index (^GSPTSE)

Date	Close	Change	% Change Since Prior Week	% Change Since Peak
6/18/2008	**15,073.13**			
6/23/2008	14,355.21	–717.92	–4.76%	–4.76%
6/30/2008	14,010.39	–344.82	–2.40%	–7.05%
7/7/2008	13,709.10	–301.29	–2.15%	–9.05%
7/14/2008	13,515.96	–193.14	–1.41%	–10.33%
7/21/2008	13,378.81	–137.15	–1.01%	–11.24%
7/28/2008	13,496.53	117.72	0.88%	–10.46%
8/5/2008	13,341.74	–154.79	–1.15%	–11.49%
8/11/2008	13,096.70	–245.04	–1.84%	–13.11%
8/18/2008	13,447.29	350.59	2.68%	–10.79%
8/25/2008	13,771.25	323.96	2.41%	–8.64%
9/2/2008	12,816.42	–954.83	–6.93%	–14.97%
9/8/2008	12,769.58	–46.84	–0.37%	–15.28%
9/15/2008	12,912.99	143.41	1.12%	–14.33%
9/22/2008	12,126.00	–786.99	–6.09%	–19.55%
9/29/2008	10,803.35	–1,322.65	–10.91%	–28.33%
10/6/2008	9,065.16	–1,738.19	–16.09%	–39.86%
10/14/2008	9,562.49	497.33	5.49%	–36.56%
10/20/2008	9,294.09	–268.40	–2.81%	–38.34%
10/27/2008	9,762.76	468.67	5.04%	–35.23%
11/3/2008	9,596.21	–166.55	–1.71%	–36.34%
11/10/2008	9,055.96	–540.25	–5.63%	–39.92%
11/17/2008	8,155.39	–900.57	–9.94%	–45.89%

Source: Yahoo! Canada Finance.

the hard-earned savings she was counting on to help send her kids to university and for her own retirement?

Tell her to sell and realize her losses with the associated insult that she'd have to pay deferred sales charges on her mutual funds to the advisor that steered her wrong in the first place?

Or maybe, tell her to hold on? That the stock market will come back eventually as it always used to?

WHAT'S NEXT?

Well, chances are the S&P/TSX index will eventually rise to the levels seen in the summer of 2008, but the $64,000 question is "How long will that take?"

Sorry, I have no idea, but let's look at it from another angle. How many years will it take to get back to the peak, assuming it recovers by 8% a year? Any idea?

The answer is, eight years. Eight years just to break even. Check it out for yourself on a calculator. Enter the index value of 8,155.39 (the value on November 17, 2008) and multiply by 1.08. You get 8,807.82. Multiply by 1.08 again and again until you get 15,073.13—the value at the peak on June 18, 2008. It takes eight times.

What if the stock market doesn't return to the average rates of the past? What if we'll only make 5% a year on average? It will take almost thirteen years to break even.

This is another perfect example of the risk of ignoring point number one of personal finances—Avoid Personal Financial Disasters.

So if this can happen in Canada, what is the answer? For me, the answer is to swear to never let it happen again. And that can only be achieved by ignoring the stock market, mutual funds and equities of any kind when it comes to personal finances.

Yes, you read that correctly. No more sleepless nights worrying about what is going to happen tomorrow. Put an end to making the investment industry rich off your hard work. Keep what you earn and never again let it evaporate into thin air.

And this book will tell you how to do it.

WHAT CAUSED THE MELTDOWN

The blame gets laid on the U.S. subprime mortgage crisis. For years in the U.S., aggressive mortgage companies pushed mortgages on U.S. consumers who could not afford them. The mortgage sellers would make fees from getting the mortgages in place regardless of the chances of future payment. Combine this with consumers anxious to keep up with the Joneses and you've got a toxic brew.

There was even a new thing created: "stated income" mortgages. This allowed people to apply for mortgages based on just filling in a form stating how much their income was. There was no checking to see if they really did earn what they said they did. A new term came about for these mortgages: "liar loans."

It was great while it lasted—mortgage grantors made good commissions and fees. Consumers maxed out the amount they could borrow based on ever-rising housing prices. They spent the money on whatever they wanted. Retailers, car manufacturers and dealers loved it, too. But when U.S. house prices started to fall, the wheels came off.

Huge mortgage companies—the main U.S. ones are called Fannie Mae and Freddie Mac—began to realize that there was no way they would ever recover a lot of the money loaned to people that could not afford their mortgages. The U.S. government was forced to step in and guarantee these companies would not fail.

The U.S. investment banks that had gotten into the act by repackaging these "toxic" mortgages and re-selling them to other investors in the U.S. and around the world began to realize that their own investments were worth a lot less than they paid for them. One of them, Lehman Brothers Holdings Inc., went bankrupt. All the others were forced to be bought out by another regular bank or, in the case of Morgan Stanley and Goldman Sachs Group Inc., converted into traditional deposit-taking banks.

Merrill Lynch & Co., Inc. was bought by Bank of America in an all-stock deal worth US$50 billion. The deal values Merrill Lynch at US$29 a share—a 70% premium to its share value at the time—although it had been trading as high as US$50 in May 2008 and US$90 a share at the beginning of January 2007.

If you look at their consolidated balance sheet at June 27, 2008 (unaudited), which I am right now, it's not hard to see why Merrill Lynch was in trouble.

They had US$966 billion in total assets and US$931 billion in total liabilities, leaving total shareholders' equity of US$35 billion. The problem lies in the fact that a lot of the assets were considered "trading assets," that are required to be listed at fair market value for accounting purposes as follows:

Derivative contracts	$86 billion
Mortgages, debt, and asset-backed	$29 billion
Goodwill and other intangible assets	$5 billion

These three items of the twenty different types of assets on their balance sheet are not the type of things you can simply cash in to pay your bills. They are complex instruments that fluctuate in value. After things began going south, it didn't take long for the decline in the asset values to exceed shareholders' equity—the entire value of the company. Merrill and the other investment banks essentially became insolvent.

THE VICIOUS SPIRAL

Please take what I've got to say in context. I am not a macro-economic theory expert. I have not studied world finance or even worked in the banking sector. I am just a simple-minded accountant, but I think we've got a huge problem here and it's not just about the stock market.

The problem we have now is not going to go away quickly. The way I see it is that reality has finally caught up with traditional economic theory. In other words, the laws of physics have caught up with the laws of economics. Let me explain.

The old formula saw lots of financially educated people make lots of money by designing complicated financial products to sell to people that didn't understand them. They took huge bonuses as they made money for their firms.

For example, it has been reported that the management of Merrill Lynch in the U.S. decided to hand out million-dollar bonuses in 2008 earlier than usual—just before they were forced to be bought out by the Bank of America to avoid going under. There were apparently about seven hundred senior staff recipients. The total has been estimated at US$3.6 billion—during a quarter when the company lost over US$15 billion. Many of these recipients were the same staff that took the risks that pretty well brought down the company. That is just sickening.

But where was the value in what these financial types were doing? Who was paying the fees on all this complex investing activity? Wasn't it the little guy or gal who invested his or her money in the market, or took out a mortgage on their home?

Didn't that million-dollar bonus come out of the pocket of the person who worked hard every day at a job making $20 per hour? The guy sweating it out on the assembly line? The girl running her own business selling clothing? The person cutting lawns and plowing driveways for a living?

It doesn't make a lot of sense to me. Eventually, when greed drives a sufficient number of people to want to make more and more money each and every year off the little guy or gal, you end up breaking the little guy or gal's back. And that is what has happened in the U.S.

The person who had a house worth, say, $200,000, and mortgaged it to the hilt to spend and try and invest, has seen the value of the home plunge. Many owe more than the house is worth now. If they had a retirement fund, it too has plunged in value. And now, their jobs are at risk. It's a perfect storm—a big one.

In Canada, we are in better shape than many Americans. We are a more conservative nation and the "get rich at all costs" mantra is not as deeply ingrained in our genes. Having said that, we still have problems: who knows how long it will take for the TSX to recover? What shall we do about our retirement portfolios now that they have tanked? What about our jobs—will the North American automobile companies even survive?

It's going to be a tough journey but there is hope. Let's build that hope on a solid foundation.

Let's forget the stock market. Don't buy another mutual fund. Sleep at night knowing your investments will NEVER decline.

Instead, live life without reading about stock market gyrations, the criminal CEO that reduced their company to a shell of its former self in the quest for personal riches, or the scam artist who sold out his clients with a get-rich-quick scheme.

WHO WANTS TO BE RICH?

You want to be rich, right? Get all the cool toys whenever you want. Take five vacations a year. Own a luxury car. But what does it take to get rich? It usually takes risk.

Are you willing to literally risk everything to get rich? Would you risk your house, the ability to pay for your kids' education, your ability to buy food when you retire? Well, that is what you are essentially doing if you put all your eggs in the stock market basket.

Those that wanted to get rich easily and borrowed to invest in the stock market have been particularly hard-hit. There was even a book out there encouraging this scheme. It told people how they could "make their mortgage tax deductible." The idea was that every time you made a mortgage payment, you would immediately take the principal repayment portion and borrow that amount to invest in mutual funds. Essentially you would never pay down your mortgage. The value of your house would eventually equal the amount you put into the mutual funds.

Investment dealers loved this idea. The main proponent of this scheme was able to charge speaker fees of thousands of dollars to help convince the unwary to sign up and begin flowing money each and every week to the investment advisors.

I feel very sorry for those people now. With housing prices declining and the value of mutual funds plunging, the risk of the strategy has become all too clear. Many people have put their personal financial lives at risk, and some could lose their homes.

This scheme violates another one of the six points, which we'll get into later: buy your house and pay it off before you retire.

If you want to take a risk in an attempt to get rich, don't do it with the funds you'll need to raise your kids and don't do it with the funds you'll need to ensure you can eat when you no longer work—just buy a lottery ticket. I'm serious. Take two dollars and buy a Lotto 649 ticket. You may get rich but if not, all you've lost is a toonie, not your home or your future.

WHY YOU DON'T NEED STOCKS

The stock market can be a great way to get wealthy. How else can you double or triple your money without any effort on your part? The problem is that it is risky. You are just as likely to end up losing your money. Think about the people who picked the wrong companies in the past and lost everything. Those who trusted Enron, WorldCom, or more recently Lehman Brothers, Washington Mutual, and their ilk.

Even if you only invest in solid companies with established earnings, excellent products and revolutionary new ideas, you could lose big time. Take Apple Computers (NASDAQ: AAPL), for example. They have recently produced the iPod music and video player and the iPhone, in addition to award-winning computers like the MacBook Pro notebook and the iMac—all incredible products that consumers want.

What has their share price done recently? Here's a chart showing month-end share prices from December 2007 to January 2009:

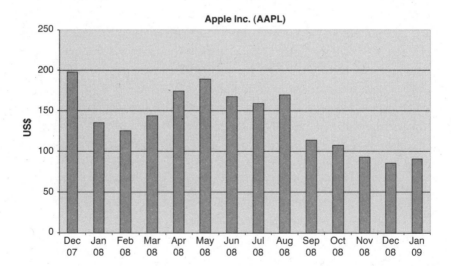

Apple's stock price peaked on December 28, 2007 at US$199.83. On January 9, 2009 it closed at US$90.58. That's a decline of US$109.25 or 55%. And that was during a period when it was making good money.

For the twelve months ended September 30, 2007, its revenues were US$24.006 billion and its net income was US$3.496 billion. The year ended September 30, 2008 saw revenues increase to US$32.479 billion and net income grow to US$4.834 billion. That was a 35% increase in revenue and a 38% increase in net income. The fact that Apple's stock price dropped so much defies logic. But that's the point—the stock market is not very logical. It's driven by emotion and feelings, not common sense.

WHY YOU DON'T NEED MUTUAL FUNDS

Mutual funds were invented to allow the individual investor access to a diversified portfolio of investments that is managed by a professional money manager. They therefore avoid the potential disaster associated with picking the wrong individual company.

OK, so your risk is reduced because with a mutual fund you'll own a number of different companies. But there are still significant other risks. I am looking at a prospectus for a mutual fund that I was personally invested in. It is a bond fund with a well-known investment company whose name you would recognize in an instant.

Current regulations require these companies to disclose the different types of risks an investor faces when they make purchases. The prospectus begins the section on risk by stating that mutual funds own different types of investments depending on their investment objectives and that the value of the investments a mutual fund owns will vary from day to day because of changes in interest rates and economic conditions, as well as market and company news. The result is that the value of any mutual fund's units may go up or down by the time you redeem it.

It further goes on to state that the full amount of any investment in their mutual funds is not guaranteed and that "unlike bank accounts or GICs, mutual fund units and shares are not covered by the Canada Deposit Insurance Corporation (CDIC) or any other government deposit insurer."

Talk about risk! If your mutual fund company happens to go under, don't bother calling the CDIC—they can't help.

The prospectus also indicates that their mutual funds may invest in different classes of securities, including bonds, equities and cash, depending on the specific fund's objectives. For example, a fund with an objective of long-term capital gain will invest mostly in equities, whereas a fund whose aim is to preserve capital will invest mostly in bonds and money market securities.

As a result, different mutual funds will carry different types of risks depending on the securities they own. The following is a long list of the eighteen types of risk you expose yourself to, depending on the specific mutual funds you invest in.

MUTUAL FUND RISKS

WARNING: The following list is long and boring, but if you own mutual funds you have to understand each and every one of them!

1. Credit Risk

This is the risk that a company that issues a bond or other fixed-income security won't be able to repay the principal or interest when it comes due. Generally, you'll put yourself at less risk if the issuer has a high credit rating from an independent credit rating agency. And, the prices of securities with higher ratings tend to be less volatile than those with lower ratings.

2. Derivative Risk

Some funds have the leeway to use derivatives—in essence, contracts that gamble on the future prices of assets—often using them in an attempt to avoid risk. The fund's description will tell you if it does. So it may seem odd that derivatives themselves have their own kinds of risk, including that the use of derivatives for hedging may not be effective, that some derivatives may limit a fund's potential for gains and not just losses, and that you, Joe Investor, may have to pay for the cost of entering and maintaining derivative contracts through reductions in the fund's total return. And that's just for starters.

3. Emerging Markets Risk

Emerging markets . . . sounds alluring, doesn't it? But the potential for earning a strong return from developing economies is offset by their smaller securities markets, which make it more difficult to sell securities to take profits or avoid losses; their lower regulation standards;

their political instability and possible corruption; and the difficulty of determining the true value of a company.

4. Equity Risk

Very simply, if a basket of stocks or shares rises in market value, then the funds that invest in it rise as well. So, strong economy begets positive company outlook begets generally rising share prices. And weak economy begets lacklustre or negative company outlook begets generally falling share prices. And there's no crystal ball telling us which way the economy is headed.

5. Foreign Currency Risk

The value of securities that are issued in foreign currencies and that earn income in foreign funds is affected by the value of the Canadian dollar relative to those currencies. For example, if the value of the foreign currency declined relative to the Canadian dollar, so too would the value of the foreign securities.

6. Foreign Equity Risk

Investments across the border, any border, are risky because of possible political or social instability, lack of information about foreign companies, and possibly lower standards of government supervision and regulation than in Canada. And, if the fund runs into trouble, it may have difficulty pursuing legal action in jurisdictions outside Canada.

7. Interest Rate Risk

The interest rate on a bond is set when it's issued. If interest rates fall, the price of an existing bond will rise because it's paying a higher rate than newer bonds and is therefore more valuable. Conversely, if interest rates rise, the value of an existing bond and any fund holding such bonds will fall. Funds that include convertible securities also carry interest rate risk.

8. Large Investor Risk

Large investors, such as financial institutions, may redeem or purchase securities of a fund. Their actions may be substantial enough to force the portfolio manager to change significantly the composition of the portfolio or to buy or sell investments at unfavourable prices, which can negatively affect return.

9. Liquidity Risk

Securities with a limited trading market have liquidity risk. Because they're difficult to sell, if supply outweighs demand for them they may trade at an amount lower than their value. To mitigate this risk, many funds set a limit for "illiquid securities."

10. Low-Rated Security Risk

Some companies offer a higher rate of return because they carry a higher risk. They may have a credit rating below investment grade or perhaps be unrated. These investments may be hard to value because market quotations aren't available and they may be less liquid than higher-grade investments. They have the potential for large gains or losses.

11. Regulatory Risk

Industries such as health care and telecommunications are heavily regulated and may receive government funding. Changes in government policy such as deregulation or reduced government funding may substantially affect companies in these sectors, so funds that buy these investments may rise and fall substantially.

12. Repurchase/Reverse Repurchase Agreements Risk

A repurchase agreement involves selling a security at one price and simultaneously agreeing to buy it back at a lower price. A reverse repurchase agreement involves buying a security at one price and simultaneously agreeing to sell it back at a higher price. This creates lots of risks. Funds then jump through hoops to reduce those risks, by holding offsetting collateral, and putting in place a series of conditions for these transactions.

13. RSP Fund Risk

RSP funds use forward contracts, debt-like securities and other specified derivatives as part of their investment strategy, which involves some specific risks in addition to the general risks of derivatives themselves. For one thing, if the underlying fund to an RSP fund runs into trouble and suspends redemptions, the corresponding RSP fund will be unable to value part of its portfolio or redeem units. Then what? And, there's the cost of the derivatives, which is borne by the RSP fund itself and eats into the returns of the RSP fund, and potential problems surrounding counterparties. Starting to feel tense yet?

14. Securities Lending Risk

Some funds can lend a portion of its portfolio securities to a qualified borrower or borrowers that have posted collateral for a fee and a set period of time. These funds run the risk that a borrower may not fulfill its obligations, leaving the fund holding collateral worth less than the securities it has lent, and resulting in a loss to the fund. To limit this risk, a cap is set on how much and what type of collateral can be held, on how much the fund can lend through such transactions, and on how much exposure it can have to any one borrower.

15. Series Risk

Your fund may have several series of units, each with its own fees and expenses, which are tracked separately from other series. If one series can't pay its portion of expenses based on its proportionate share of the fund assets, another series may have to help out. If your fund is the one helping out its down-on-luck brother, your investment return is probably going to suffer.

16. Smaller Company Risk

The stock price of smaller companies is often more volatile than that of larger, more established companies. This is because they may be developing new products that haven't been tested in the marketplace, their existing products quickly become obsolete, they usually have limited access to funding, and they may suffer from inexperienced management, not to mention that they usually trade in smaller volumes and less frequently than larger company shares so any share purchase or sale has a greater impact on their share price.

17. Tax Class Fund Risk

While assets and liabilities of each Tax Class Fund are tracked separately, the investment company, Tax Class Corp., as a whole is responsible for all of the financial obligations of the Tax Class Funds combined. If a Tax Class Fund cannot pay its expenses using its proportionate share of the assets, the investment company, Tax Class Corp., may have to pay those expenses out of the other Tax Class Funds' assets, which could lower the investment return of those other Tax Class Funds. As well, the tax consequences of an investment in a Tax Class Fund will depend in part on the tax position of the investment company, Tax Class Corp., as a whole and will differ from an investment in a mutual fund that is not part of a multi-class structure.

18. Underlying Fund Risk

The investment company and unaffiliated third parties may offer investment products that use a "fund on fund" structure whereby a "top fund" invests all or a significant portion of its assets in a "bottom" or "underlying fund." Depending on the size of the investment being made by a top fund in an underlying fund and the timing of the redemption of this investment, an underlying fund could be forced to alter significantly its portfolio assets to accommodate a large redemption order, having a negative impact on the performance of the underlying fund.

That's a lot of risk isn't it? Well, if you own mutual funds, you need to be aware of and understand the ins and outs of every one of these different types of risks.

THOSE DARNED MUTUAL FUND FEES!

OK. We've established that mutual funds are risky and have learned the hard way that they can fall significantly and quickly. But there is another huge reason you don't need mutual funds: excessive, draining and hidden fees.

Oh, thank you—the mutual fund prospectus I'm looking at has a whole section titled "Fees and Expenses." Let's have a look, shall we?

It starts off by noting that some of the fees are paid directly by you and that others are "payable by the funds or portfolios, which will indirectly reduce the value of your investment in the fund or portfolio." In other words, some you'll see taken directly out of your investment account and some will be taken out of the pool of money you have contributed to.

Let's start with the section on fees and expenses payable directly by you:

1. Fees and Expenses Payable Directly by You
Sales Charges

Most mutual fund companies divide their offerings into different "series" of units and the one we have been talking about is no exception. In this case they are either "front load" or "rear load."

Front-Load Option

You pay up to 6% of the purchase price, as negotiated between you and your dealer.

Interesting observation: many of the fees your investment advisor charges you are negotiable. Did you know that?

Rear-Load (Deferred Sales Charge) Option

In all likelihood, you have never purchased a front-load type fund. The usual line from the salespeople is "Why would you? You'd like all your money working for you, wouldn't you?"

So they convince you that the rear-load, or deferred sales charge (DSC), option is the best.

Under this option, you pay a redemption fee if you redeem your units within a certain number of years of buying them—up to six years, in this company's case. Here's the scale of fees:

- 6.0% in the first year after purchase
- 5.5% in the second year
- 5.0% in the third year
- 4.5% in the fourth year
- 4.0% in the fifth year
- 3.0% in the sixth year
- nil after six years

The redemption fee may be based on the original cost of the units or the market value when you cash them in. In this company's case, it's the original cost. In declining stock markets this can really add insult to injury. Say you purchased $10,000 of the DSC series of the equity fund before the market crash of 2008. Your $10,000 tanked to $6,000 and you'd like to get out. The cost to sell and realize the $4,000 loss before it gets worse? It's 6% of $10,000, or $600. Ouch.

Switch Fees

It will cost up to 2% as negotiated between you and your dealer to change funds.

Short-Term Trading Fees

You'll pay up to 2% if you request to switch out of any fund within two weeks of an earlier switch request, switch more than twice within a 90-day period or "appear to follow a market timing pattern that may adversely affect a fund or portfolio."

Registered Plan Fees Payable to the Trustee

Such fees include semi-annual trustee fees for Registered Education Savings Plans (RESPs; $7.50 in this case), other registered plans (0.20% of account value, minimum $7.50, maximum $25) and RSP redemption fees ($15 per redemption plus any deferred sales charge).

Other Fees

These fees include bank wiring costs for wiring redemption proceeds to your account.

2. Fees and Expenses Payable by the Fund or Portfolio
Management Fees

Management fees are paid by the mutual funds to the investment manager for investment management and general administrative services. A portion of the management fees are sales commissions and trail fees paid to dealers who bring in the clients' money.

The prospectus I am looking at states that they paid dealers 56% of the total management fees they earned on all funds and portfolios and that "this amount included sales commissions and trail fees as well as our support of their promotional activities." Do you know what that means? It means current investors are paying so the mutual fund managers can attract more clients. That's a sweet deal—for them.

Just what are "trail fees?" They're fees, usually ranging from 0.5% to 1.0% per year, that are paid to your dealer as long as you own the funds. This is for the ongoing advice they are supposed to be providing you. Are you getting your money's worth? In many cases the answer is no. Sometimes, advisors don't even return your phone calls!

And here's another interesting tidbit: Even with a DSC mutual fund where you, as the investor, do not pay a front-load fee, this particular company pays the dealer a sales commission of 5% of the amount you invested, through the management expenses. But you'll still be subject to the redemption fee if you cash out within six years. Talk about having your cake and eating it, too!

And another one: They may reduce the management expenses for certain investors. Their decision depends on the size and nature of the investment. In other words, the big guys like pension funds, insurers and other institutional investors get a discount on fees. You, small fry, don't.

Operating Expenses

Mutual funds are like large companies. They have infrastructures that have to be maintained and that costs money. Here is a list of the operating expenses that the funds have to pay:

- legal
- audit
- custodial
- registrar and transfer agent fees
- bank fees and expenses
- cost of preparing financial statements, prospectuses and other reports
- other administrative expenses
- taxes

The Management Expense Ratio

You may be familiar with the term "management expense ratio" (MER), as it is often discussed in the media when it comes to the cost of owning mutual funds. The MER shows how much a fund paid in management fees and operating expenses (including goods and services tax) during a year. It is expressed as an annualized percentage of the daily average net assets during the year.

Generally, the MER for equity-based mutual funds is higher than for fixed-income or bond funds because choosing and monitoring hundreds of different companies' shares is more labour-intensive than choosing a series of fixed-income securities.

If you invest in mutual funds, you should know what the MER is for each and every one. In Canada, the typical equity-based mutual fund MER is above 2%. The Globefund.com database yields an average MER of 2.75% for Canadian equity mutual funds based on 2004 data.

Ever wonder why it seems you never manage to get ahead with Canadian equity mutual funds, even when the stock market is heading the right way? Fees, fees and more fees!

THE PUKE POINT

The Puke Point is that point in an investor's life when it all just becomes too much. You can't help but regurgitate all of your remaining stocks and mutual funds and resolve never to own another one. (No, I didn't invent that term, but I wish I had!)

But there is a problem when it comes to getting rid of your mutual funds: it could cost you a huge amount of money. The brilliance of the creators of mutual funds now becomes even more evident.

Not only have they guaranteed their constant annual income through visible and hidden fees even when your investment value goes down, they make it very costly for you to leave.

Let's look at a simple example. I have used a common Canadian equity mutual fund purchased on January 1, 2008 and sold on December 31, 2008. It is an actual DSC fund of the investment company whose prospectus I have been talking about.

The net asset value (NAV) per unit on January 1, 2008 was $69.93. Let's say we had $10,000 and we therefore bought 143 units (143 units × $69.93 each = $10,000). Since this is a DSC fund, the full $10,000 was invested and showed on our investment statement in January.

As we know, our investment advisor got his sales commission of 5% of $10,000. He got $500 out of the pot of money the mutual fund had from all investors like us. That fee is reflected in the annual return of the mutual fund, which affects the ending value of the mutual fund.

The NAV of this mutual fund actually rose to $76 in May of 2008, but the value on December 31, 2008 was only $49.66. The value of our investment on December 31, 2008 was therefore $7,101.38 (143 units × $49.66 each). In that one year we lost $2,898.62, or 29% of our money.

But at this point it's an unrealized loss. We could hold on and hope things get better. But let's say we've had enough and want to limit our losses to 29%. What is the cost to redeem our units? Well, it's that ugly DSC fee of 6.0% in the first year after purchase. And it's on the original value of the investment—$10,000 in this case.

Kiss goodbye another $600.

The amount of money we'll get out is only $6,501.38. That's the $7,101.38 our investment value had declined to, less the $600 DSC fee.

Our total loss was $3,498.62—35% of our original investment.

HOW TO GET RID OF YOUR "DOG" FUNDS

The irony of getting to a 100% safe investment strategy is that getting out of the losing mutual funds you have accumulated over the years is the hardest part because it is so costly.

My advice would be not to overreact and dump them all at once. It's probably best to take an organized approach to getting to safety. It's also not a good idea to just dump your investment advisor at this stage. You'll need him or her to help make the changes you'll want to make.

Step #1: The 10% Peel

The first step is to realize that you are allowed to redeem up to 10% of a mutual fund in each calendar year without paying a redemption fee. Start by instructing your advisor to do this for each of the funds you'd like to get rid of. It's not quick, but at least it's a start.

Step #2: What'll It Cost Me to Get Out?

The second step is to ask your advisor to get the following information for each of the mutual funds you own:

- the DSC redemption charge you will pay to cash in the fund as of a certain date
- the date the fund will be "DSC free" or cashable with no redemption fee

Once you've assembled all the information, you'll have a decision to make on each fund.

You may be lucky enough to have some funds that you have held long enough that there will be no DSC fee. In other cases, the fee may be small enough that you'll be willing to take the hit and pay the fee just to get rid of the fund.

In still other cases, you may think it best to hold on for another year or two in the hopes that the market comes back. In this case, make sure that you have confidence in the fund manager who will be making the important decisions in the fund over whatever period you are going to hold on to it for.

The key recommendation is to be patient. It took years to get into the mess you are in. It's best not to try and get out in one day.

A WORD ABOUT LABOUR-SPONSORED INVESTMENT FUNDS

Labour-Sponsored Investment Funds (LSIFs) were created to give a special tax break for people willing to invest in start-up Canadian businesses through special mutual funds. The break is given because there is a high risk that many of the start-ups won't survive. Some of the investments will have to be written off, which will affect the funds' rates of return.

It's the possibility of a star company emerging that makes them more attractive. For example, Research in Motion, maker of the BlackBerry, was originally an LSIF.

The problem is that the majority of these investment companies have a short history and most are not publicly traded. It is therefore difficult to value them. They also have high MERs—in many cases more than 4%.

LSIFs were very popular in the 1990s because of generous federal and provincial tax breaks and some initial good returns. The tax breaks have been scaled back in recent years, however, and the returns of these funds overall has been unimpressive—negative in many cases.

Most people (me included) originally got into LSIFs for the tax breaks. The federal government used to offer a 20% tax credit (that has been reduced to 15%) on the first $5,000 invested in an LSIF. Most provinces offer an additional 15% credit. This added up to quite the tax break, especially for LSIFs held in an RRSP account. For example, if you were in the 40% marginal tax bracket you'd get a $2,000 income tax refund on the $5,000 RRSP contribution, a $750 tax credit from the federal government and $750 from the provincial one. Your $5,000 contribution cost you only $1,500 ($5,000 – $2,000 – $750 – $750).

The catch is that you have to hold onto the investments for eight years (five years if purchased before 1996); otherwise, you'll have to pay those juicy tax credits back.

If you own some LSIFs, find out when you'll be free from paying back the tax credits.

WE WON'T GET SCREWED AGAIN

OK, let's begin the journey to a safe, comfortable retirement. We've agreed to swear off the stock market and mutual funds and never blindly trust another person, be it a stranger, a relative or a friend, to handle our hard-earned savings. Well, what *do* we put our money in?

We only put it in fixed-income products that can NEVER decline in value. That basically means GICs (guaranteed investment certificates), term deposits or high-income savings accounts. We also don't trust all the financial institutions, so we have to make sure they are all 100% guaranteed by the federal government. That means we need to find out all there is to know about the Canada Deposit Insurance Corporation (CDIC).

The Canada
Deposit Insurance Corporation

We are going to invest only in things that are guaranteed never to lose their value but we also want to make sure they are insured if the issuer goes bust.

In Canada, the CDIC was created by parliament in 1967 as a federal Crown corporation. The CDIC insures Canadians' savings should their bank or other CDIC member institution fail or go bankrupt. It is not a bank or an insurance company.

You don't need to sign up for the insurance and you don't need to pay for it, either. The CDIC is funded by fees from the member institutions.

While banks in Canada seldom fail, they can and do. Take a guess how many Canadian institutions have failed and had to be bailed out by the CDIC. My guess was a dozen. The real number? Forty-three.

Yes, that's right. Since the CDIC was created in 1967, forty-three institutions have failed. Here's the list posted at http://www.cdic.ca/1/7/0/7/index1.shtml. Hopefully you don't recognize any:

CDIC Member Institution	Year of Failure
Commonwealth Trust Company	1970
Security Trust Company Limited	1972
Astra Trust Company	1980
District Trust Company	1982
AMIC Mortgage Investment Corporation	1983
Crown Trust Company	1983
Fidelity Trust Company	1983
Greymac Mortgage Corporation	1983

Greymac Trust Company	1983
Seaway Mortgage Corporation	1983
Seaway Trust Company	1983
Northguard Mortgage Corporation	1984
CCB Mortgage Investment Corporation	1985
Canadian Commercial Bank	1985
Continental Trust Company	1985
London Loan Limited	1985
Northland Bank	1985
Pioneer Trust Company	1985
Western Capital Trust Company	1985
Bank of British Columbia	1986
Bank of British Columbia Mortgage Corporation	1986
Columbia Trust Company	1986
North West Trust Company	1987
Principal Savings & Trust Company	1987
Financial Trust Company	1988
Settlers Savings and Mortgage Corporation	1990
Bank of Credit and Commerce Canada	1991
Saskatchewan Trust Company	1991
Standard Loan Company	1991
Standard Trust Company	1991
Shoppers Trust Company	1992
Central Guaranty Mortgage Corporation	1992
Central Guaranty Trust Company	1992
First City Trust Company	1992
First City Mortgage Company	1992
Dominion Trust Company	1993
Prenor Trust Company of Canada	1993
Confederation Trust Company	1994
Monarch Trust Company	1994
Income Trust Company	1995
North American Trust Company	1995
NAL Mortgage Company	1995
Security Home Mortgage Corporation	1996

What the CDIC Covers

The CDIC only insures certain types of investments, as follows:

- savings and chequing accounts
- GICs and other term deposits that mature in five years or less
- money orders, certified cheques, traveller's cheques and bank drafts issued by CDIC members (that are payable to you and not yet cashed)
- debentures (only those issued by loan companies)

What the CDIC Does Not Cover

It does not insure these:

- mutual funds
- stocks
- GICs and other term deposits that mature in more than five years
- bonds
- treasury bills
- any accounts or products in U.S. dollars or any other foreign currency

It should be noted that these rules apply even if your investments are in a Registered Retirement Savings Plan (RRSP) or Registered Retirement Income Fund (RRIF). For example, if your RRSP is with a CDIC member institution but all it holds is mutual funds, you are not insured. That includes money market mutual funds.

The CDIC also only insures Canadian dollar deposits in debentures that are issued by a loan company that is a CDIC member. CDIC does not insure debentures issued by governments or other corporations.

The CDIC does not cover losses due to fraud, theft or scams.

The CDIC Can Cover More Than $100,000

Here's some good news: the CDIC insures up to $100,000 in up to six categories at one institution. Here's the list:

1. **In the name of one depositor**—for example, a person, business or other organization

2. **In joint names**—for example, married couples or business partners

3. **A trust account**—an account set up by a trustee for a beneficiary (e.g., a grandmother setting up a savings account for a grandchild to use later)

4. **An RRSP**—a Registered Retirement Savings Account

5. **A RRIF**—a Registered Retirement Income Fund; an account that regularly pays you after you retire

6. **A realty tax account**—deposits made towards realty taxes on mortgaged properties

So, if you had $100,000 in one of each of these accounts at a single CDIC member institution, fully $600,000 would be covered by the CDIC.

List of CDIC Members

Make sure your financial institution is a member of the CDIC by checking the CDIC website (http://www.cdic.ca). Here is the list of members as of May 2009:

AGF Trust Company
Amex Bank of Canada
B2B Trust
Bank of China (Canada)
Bank of East Asia (Canada)
Bank of Montreal (BMO)
Bank of Montreal Mortgage
  Corporation
Bank of Nova Scotia (Scotiabank)
Bank of Nova Scotia Trust
  Company
Bank West
BMO Trust Company
Bridgewater Bank
Caledon Trust Company
Canada Trust Company
Canadian Imperial Bank of
  Commerce (CIBC)
Canadian Tire Bank
Canadian Western Bank
Canadian Western Trust Company
CIBC Mellon Trust Company
CIBC Mortgages Inc.

CIBC Trust Corporation
Citibank Canada
Citizens Bank of Canada
Community Trust Company
Computershare Trust Company
  of Canada
Concentra Financial Services
  Association
Concentra Trust
CS Alterna Bank
CTC Bank of Canada
Desjardins Trust Inc.
DirectCash Bank
Dundee Bank of Canada
Effort Trust Company
Equitable Trust Company
First Data Loan Company, Canada
First Nations Bank of Canada
General Bank of Canada
Habib Canadian Bank
Home Trust Company
Household Trust Company
HSBC Bank Canada

HSBC Mortgage Corporation (Canada)
HSBC Trust Company (Canada)
ICICI Bank Canada
Industrial Alliance Trust Inc.
ING Bank of Canada
Investors Group Trust Co. Ltd.
Jameson Bank
Korea Exchange Bank of Canada
Laurentian Bank of Canada
Laurentian Trust of Canada Inc.
LBC Trust
League Savings & Mortgage Company
M.R.S. Trust Company
Manulife Bank of Canada
Maple Trust Company
MBNA Canada Bank
MCAN Mortgage Corporation
Mega International Commercial Bank (Canada)
Montreal Trust Company of Canada
Natcan Trust Company
National Bank of Canada
National Bank Trust Inc.
National Trust Company
Pacific & Western Bank of Canada
Peace Hills Trust Company
Peoples Trust Company
RBC Dexia Investor Services Trust
ResMor Trust Company
Royal Bank Mortgage Corporation
Royal Bank of Canada (RBC)
Royal Trust Company
Royal Trust Corporation of Canada
Scotia Mortgage Corporation
Shinhan Bank of Canada
State Bank of India (Canada)
Sun Life Financial Trust Inc.
TD Mortgage Corporation
TD Pacific Mortgage Corporation
Toronto-Dominion Bank
UBS Bank (Canada)

THE ADVANTAGES OF GICs

There are many advantages to GICs. Here are a few of them.

Easy to Understand

With a GIC, what you see is what you get. Your investment statement will show how much the GIC was purchased for, what the term is (e.g., one year, five year) and what the annual interest rate is. You'll know exactly what it will be worth at any point in time going forward. Oh, and it won't ever be worth less than you paid for it because the principal is guaranteed at maturity.

No Fees

Even if you buy a GIC through an investment advisor, any fees that he or she might earn for placing the GIC with a financial institution won't (or shouldn't!) come from the interest earned by the GIC. In other words, you should pay no up-front fee to invest in them and

ALL ABOUT GICs

A GIC is an investment security, sold by Canadian banks and trust companies, that provides a rate of return as well as a return of the principal amount at the end of its term. When purchasing a GIC, you'll need to consider the following options:

Cashable/Non-cashable

This is also known as redeemable/non-redeemable. If the GIC is cashable or redeemable you can cash in part or all of it before its maturity date, although there will usually be a penalty for doing so. Non-cashable or non-redeemable means you cannot cash it early, even if you need the funds. Thus, it is important to make sure you won't need the funds if you opt for the non-cashable type.

Interest Payment Frequency

This refers to how often interest is actually paid on a GIC. Options include monthly, annually or at the end of the term.

Compounding

Refers to how often the interest earned is added to the principal for the calculation of the next amount of interest. For example, interest could be calculated annually and paid at maturity. That means that a $1,000 GIC at 5% a year would build to a maturity value of $1,276.29 after five years. It would be worth $1,050 at the end of year one ($1,000 × 1.05%), then $1,102.50 after year two ($1,050 × 1.05%), $1,157.63 after year three ($1,102.50 × 1.05%), $1,215.51 after year four ($1,157.63 × 1.05%) and $1,276.29 after year five ($1,215.51 × 1.05%).

Market-Linked GICs

These GICs provide returns based on the performance of a certain stock market index. The return you actually earn is usually less than 100% of the return of the index (the bank or trust company has to make fees somehow!) and there may or may not be a minimum guaranteed return. In other words, if the index actually declines during the period you'd get your principal back but no interest.

Variable Rate

These GICs publish changing rates over the term of the GIC. They often start at a low rate and escalate so the final year's return looks really good but the average return is usually similar to what you could get with a fixed interest rate. Watch out for these—I recently heard of a bank that simply redeemed one of these half-way through the term—the high rates at the end looked too costly for them!

Minimum Investment Amount

This is the lowest amount you'll need to invest to open up an account.

even if the advisor gets paid a fee it does not come out of your return. This is unlike typical mutual funds, where fees can be eating away at your investment through the management expenses of the mutual fund itself—fees that you don't really see.

Flexible

It used to be that you had to lock in your funds for a fixed period of time and if you cashed early for any reason you would pay a large penalty—often any interest you had earned to date. Now there are many types and terms of cashable GICs.

Insured

As we have seen, GICs are insured by the CDIC so that if the institution where you hold your GIC (whether inside or outside an RRSP) goes under, you'll get your money back. This is not the case with mutual funds, even money-market ones.

Why They Try to Make GICs Complicated

Just like anything else, when it comes to investments, even GICs can get confusing. There are a couple of advantages to making investment products as complicated and confusing as possible. They are only advantages if you are a seller, though. To you as a buyer, complication is your enemy.

The first advantage is that fees are much easier to extract when it comes to complicated products. For example, do you really understand how equity mutual funds work? How about income trusts? They are extremely complex, risky vehicles that make it virtually impossible to figure out how much the advisors and sponsors get paid. But be assured, they do get paid, even if your investment is devastated by performance losses.

The second advantage to complexity is that it makes it difficult for you to figure out how well the investment is doing. That's because there are many excuses not to provide you with the information. "It's too complicated to figure out and even if we could, you probably wouldn't understand."

Are you kidding me? They want to put us in a product that is so complicated that they, the sellers, can't even figure out the personal rate of return? Don't believe it. They know exactly how well it's doing. They're just worried that if you knew, you'd take your money elsewhere—somewhere you could be assured you weren't getting taken.

That's why they invented things like market-linked and escalating rate GICs.

HOW AND WHY THEY BASH GICs

I am tired of seeing the following arguments against GICs:

"Sure GICs are safe, but have you ever considered the tax and inflation affects? You may even be losing money! That's because of taxes and inflation. If your GIC is earning 4% a year, you'll pay tax on the interest earned and if you are in the 46% income tax bracket, that 4% a year means you'll only earn 2.16% after paying 1.84% (4.0% × 46% tax) in taxes. Since inflation is around 2.2%, your real rate of return is actually negative 0.04%!"

This argument usually is followed by the advice to invest in the stock market. Hopefully you did not read such an article before the fall of 2008. Here's why the argument does not make sense to me.

First of all, it is correct that interest income from a GIC is taxed as normal income is, at 100%. Capital gains from the sale of stocks and mutual funds are taxed at only 50% of the gain. That's why I recommend that you hold GICs in RRSPs, RRIFs and the new Tax-Free Savings Accounts (TFSAs). In this way, you retain the full 4% rate of return, at least until you withdraw the funds in the case of RRSPs and RRIFs.

The second argument about inflation is a red herring. What does inflation have to do with investment returns? Inflation surely does have a significant effect on the price of the things you buy, but even if inflation is rising, is that a good reason to remove the safety net of the GIC principal guarantee and risk losing your money in the stock market? In other words, assume you are retired and on a fixed income and your property taxes rose 5% last year to $4,200 from $4,000, an increase of $200. Does the fact that your conservative retirement nest-egg RRIF only went up from $200,000 to $208,000, an increase of 4% before inflation, bother you?

I'll tell you what would bother me: if my $200,000 RRIF that was 50% invested in the stock market dove to $169,000. That would be the case if the $100,000 in the Canadian stock market lost $35,000 (35%) and declined to $65,000, while the other $100,000 in GICs went up to $104,000 (a 4% increase) for a total value of $169,000 ($65,000 plus $104,000).

What would you do if you sold the stock market for a living? You'd probably dream up other reasons to bash GICs, too. But you don't sell the stock market for a living, do you? Well then, if you want to get ahead, don't listen to the people that do, and avoid potential personal financial disasters.

THE LADDERED GIC

Once you do start investing, consider putting your money in a sure thing that can't lose: GICs, term deposits or high-interest savings accounts. Resolve not to pay another dime to the investment "advisors" that get rich off you behind the scenes with hidden fees and commissions while putting your retirement at risk.

A word of warning: unfortunately you can't simply switch your mutual funds for GICs even within the same RRSP with the same company. You'll still be subject to all the DSC and other fees to get out. That's because switching will mean your investment advisor and his company won't be able to soak you for huge fees anymore. They will probably try to dissuade you from switching at all costs. How are they going to be able to afford to put that second story on the Lake Rosseau cottage if you switch!?

Let's delve into the "laddered GIC" strategy of investing in short-, medium- and long-term savings vehicles to make sure cash is available when needed and to reduce the risk related to declining interest rates.

Remember, the CDIC only covers GICs and term deposits that mature in five years or less, so five years is the longest we want to buy.

Here is how the strategy works:

Step 1. Divide whatever amount you have into five.

Step 2. Invest 20% (one-fifth) in each of a one-, two-, three-, four-
and five-year GIC.

Step 3. Each year that any of the GICs mature, reinvest the proceeds in a five-year GIC at the prevailing rate.

Let's have a look at how the strategy would have worked over the
last ten years, starting in 1998.

According to the Bank of Canada (http://www.bankofcanada
.ca/en/rates/interest-look.html), from 1998 to 2008, the average GIC
rates were as follows:

Average GIC Rates, 1998–2008

	1998	1999	2000	2001	2002	2003	2004	2005	2006	2007	2008
One-year	3.62	3.83	4.67	2.64	1.62	1.71	1.19	1.53	2.78	2.98	2.14%
Three-year	4.03	4.46	5.12	3.38	2.79	2.48	2.23	2.15	2.99	3.14	2.69%
Five-year	4.38	4.81	5.34	4.05	3.91	3.13	2.92	2.71	3.16	3.31	3.05%

Let's look at the results of the laddered GIC strategy used for the
period 1998 to 2008. Have a look at the chart on the next page.

Have a look at the first strategy in the table on the next page above:
rolling over at consistent term. It shows that over the ten-year period
from 1998 to 2008, if we had simply invested in 100% government-
guaranteed GICs and rolled the one-, two-, three-, four- and five-year
GICs over at the same term each time they came due, our original
$50,000 would have grown to a value of $70,025.20. That's an average
annual rate of return of 3.43%.

This is a good strategy to use if you'll need some of the money
within five years, for example, if you are turning seventy-two and will
need to make minimum required RRIF withdrawals.

But what if your time horizon is longer than five years? What if
you'd like to use GICs in your RRSP when you have more than five
years to go before needing the money? Well, you can modify the laddered GIC strategy to benefit from the higher longer-term rates.

GIC Laddered 1998–2008

Initial investment: $50,000.00

Start Date: 1-Jun-98

End Date: 1-Jun-08

	1998	1999	2000	2001	2002	2003	2004	2005	2006	2007	2008
One-Year	3.62%	3.83%	4.67%	2.64%	1.62%	1.71%	1.19%	1.53%	2.78%	2.98%	2.14%
Two-Year	3.83%	4.15%	4.90%	3.01%	2.21%	2.10%	1.71%	1.84%	2.89%	3.06%	2.42%
Three-Year	4.03%	4.46%	5.12%	3.38%	2.79%	2.48%	2.23%	2.15%	2.99%	3.14%	2.69%
Four-Year	4.21%	4.64%	5.23%	3.72%	3.35%	2.81%	2.58%	2.43%	3.08%	3.23%	2.87%
Five-Year	4.38%	4.81%	5.34%	4.05%	3.91%	3.13%	2.92%	2.71%	3.16%	3.31%	3.05%

Strategy 1: Rolling over at consistent term

	1998	1999	2000	2001	2002	2003	2004	2005	2006	2007	2008
1	$ 10,000.00	$10,362.00	$ 10,758.86	$ 11,261.30	$ 11,558.60	$ 11,745.85	$ 11,946.71	$ 12,088.87	$ 12,273.83	$ 12,615.04	$ 12,990.97
2	$ 10,000.00		$ 10,779.63		$ 11,860.79		$ 12,389.61		$ 12,816.96		$ 13,567.17
3	$ 10,000.00			$ 11,258.38			$ 13,077.71			$ 14,075.03	$ 14,516.98
4	$ 10,000.00				$ 11,791.10				$ 13,643.33		$ 14,495.30
5	$ 10,000.00					$ 12,390.43					$ 14,454.78
	$ 50,000.00										**$ 70,025.20**

Strategy 2: Rolling over to five-year

	1998	1999	2000	2001	2002	2003	2004	2005	2006	2007	2008
1	$ 10,000.00	$10,362.00					$ 13,105.61				$ 14,704.70
2	$ 10,000.00		$ 10,779.63					$ 13,982.04			$ 15,149.86
3	$ 10,000.00			$ 11,258.38					$ 13,730.50		$ 14,611.97
4	$ 10,000.00				$ 11,791.10					$ 14,283.71	$ 14,756.50
5	$ 10,000.00					$ 12,390.43					$ 14,454.78
	$ 50,000.00										$ 73,677.82

Five-Year strategy better by: **$ 3,652.62**

Look at the second strategy: rolling over to a five-year GIC. It shows that the higher five-year rates would have grown the original $50,000 to $73,677.82. That's $3,652.62 better than Strategy 1 and represents an average annual rate of return of 3.95% a year.

GETTING THE BEST GIC RATES

Finding the best GIC interest rate is worth the effort, especially when we're talking about a longer period of time. For example, a 1% increase in the average rate of return of a $50,000 five-year GIC to 5% from 4% over a ten-year period would build your savings to $81,445—$7,432 higher than the $74,013 you'd end up with at 4%.

Example 1

$50,000 GIC, five-year term, 4% annual rate of return, compounded annually:

Value after five years = $60,833
Value after ten years = $74,013

Example 2

$50,000 GIC, five-year term, 5% annual rate of return, compounded annually:

Value after five years = $63,814
Value after ten years = $81,445

That's over $7,000 more just for finding an interest rate that's 1% better.

So where do you go to find the best rates? You don't need a fancy investment advisor that drives a Lexus. You can do it yourself. All you need is access to the Internet.

On January 6, 2009, I googled "GIC interest rates" for Canada and found the following on the websites of the big five banks for non-cashable long-term GICs eligible for RRSPs and RRIFs:

	Minimum Investment in a Five-year GIC	Interest Rate on a Five-year GIC	Website	Phone Number
CIBC	$1,000	2.6%	http://www.cibc.com/ca/rates/gic-rates.html	1-866-525-8622
TD Canada Trust	$500	2.6%	http://www.tdcanadatrust.com/GICs/GICTable.jsp	1-800-465-5463
RBC	$500	2.2%	http://www.rbcroyalbank.com/rates.rsp.html#gic	1-800-769-2511
Bank of Montreal	$1,000	2.6%	http://www4.bmo.com/termproducts/navigator/0,4739,35649_25138242,00.html	1-877-225-5266
Scotiabank	$1,000	2.6%	http://scotiabank.com/rates/gic.html	1-800-953-7441

When I called one of the banks above to get further details about the non-cashable five-year GIC rate to see if there was any flexibility in the rate, the answer was "no." The website, however, did say that I could get an "online purchase/renewal bonus" of 0.50%. The person I spoke to said this was not available if I purchased the GIC through her on the phone.

The person then began talking about the benefits of a market-linked GIC that provided returns linked to certain market index increases over the time period. She indicated one product that guaranteed a minimum of 15% over a five-year period, up to a maximum of 40%, but I could not find this product on the bank's website. All the market-linked GICs listed had a maximum return amount listed but the minimum return was zero if the associated market had a negative return.

The moral of the story is that it is a little complicated to try to do this all yourself. Your best strategy is to educate yourself in all the GIC options before you start calling to get the best product and rate. You may also wish to consider getting some help from a deposit broker.

CONSIDER A DEPOSIT BROKER

A deposit broker is an independent financial professional who specializes in guaranteed investment products such as GICs and term deposits.

I honestly knew very little about them until I started researching this book. I actually had an accounting client that utilized a deposit broker to handle their GIC investments. I always wondered why it was necessary to have a broker handle something as simple as GICs. Now I'm convinced they can play an important role in your retirement plans.

Finds the Best Rates

The first important role deposit brokers fulfill is to monitor the available interest rates of various products on a daily basis to find the best possible returns. Because different products are constantly being developed, and because demand and activity vary daily with each financial institution, new opportunities for better rates are constantly being created.

According to one deposit broker I talked to, they can often find rates that are up to 1% better than the posted rates of the financial institutions. As we have seen, that can make a huge difference in your retirement nest egg over the long term.

Saves Time

A deposit broker saves you the time and effort of finding the current rates of dozens of different financial institutions. While many investment advisors often prefer to sell mutual funds, including money market funds issued by their own company, a deposit broker is usually independent and has access to many unrelated financial institutions' rates.

Provides Advice

Even though investing in simple, no-risk GICs is not as complex as the typical mutual fund, it is still important to get independent advice on their use. For example, for estate planning purposes you might decide the right registration is jointly with your spouse instead of in your name only. You may also need advice on what terms to renew at as you approach the age where you will need access to your money. You may also wish to have another person double-check to make sure you are onside with respect to CDIC insurance limits.

You Don't Pay Fees

When purchasing GICs and other guaranteed investments through a deposit broker, you don't pay fees or commissions to your broker. There are also no "hidden fees" being taken out of your investment returns, as is the case with mutual funds through the management expenses. Deposit brokers do get paid, however—they receive a finder's fee directly from the institutions that they purchase the GICs from.

WHO REGULATES DEPOSIT BROKERS?

In Canada, the self-regulatory organization for deposit brokers is the Registered Deposit Brokers Association (RDBA), formerly known as the Federation of Canadian Independent Deposit Brokers (FCIDB). The RDBA regulates the operations and business conduct of its members and their representatives in order to protect investors and the public interest.

Incorporated in 1987 and given the mandate in late 2008 to represent the industry, the RDBA is responsible for representing and organizing the industry's views, developing policies and procedures for dealing with the regulatory requirements, and for auditing member firm compliance with the rules.

According to an RDBA media release dated December 1, 2008:

> Nationally, across Canada, an estimated 3,500 individuals act as or on behalf of a Deposit Broker, helping investors find the best rates for Guaranteed Investment Certificates (GICs) and other guaranteed deposit products issued by banks, trust companies and other financial institutions. Approximately $30 billion in such deposits are placed each year through this independent broker network with oversight left to each Financial Institution's independent effort. The necessity of more than 30 [financial institutions], each complying with stringent Know Your Client (KYC) and product disclosure best practices and the various legislative acts such as AML&ATF (Money laundering), PIPEDA (Privacy) and product disclosure, places a heavy burden in administration and costs on all industry stakeholders. (Registered Deposit Brokers Association, Deposit Industry Commits to Self-Regulation. http://www.rdba.ca/news/press/pr_20081201.htm.)

Remember that not all of the financial institutions represented by the broker are members of CDIC. Insurance companies are covered by Assuris (a not-for-profit organization that protects Canadian policyholders in the event that their life insurance company should fail) and credit unions are covered by their provincial deposit insurance organization.

Also beware that not all deposit brokers are registered members of the RDBA and bound by its policies and procedures and code of ethics.

FISCAL AGENTS

Fiscal Agents Financial Services Group (http://www.fiscalagents.com) is a deposit broker registered with the RDBA. In fact, Fiscal Agents' founder, David Newman, was instrumental in convincing the federal government to increase the CDIC insurance coverage of bank and trust company deposits to $100,000 from $60,000.

You may have seen Fiscal Agents' charts of maximum GIC rates in the *National Post*, the *Toronto Star* or on several finance-related websites.

Here is a summary chart that the company prepares for clients based on a review of many financial institutions' published rates, generated on January 6, 2009:

Institution	Minimum Investment in a Five-year GIC	Interest Rate on a Five-year GIC	Insured by CDIC?
Chartered Banks			
Alterna Bank-Savings	$500	3.60%	No
AMEX	$1,000	3.50%	Yes
Bank of Montreal	$1,000	2.60%	Yes
Bank of Nova Scotia	$1,000	2.60%	Yes
Canadian Tire Bank	$500	4.00%	Yes
Canadian Western Bank	$1,000	3.85%	Yes
CIBC	$1,000	2.60%	Yes
Citibank Canada	$5,000	2.35%	Yes
Citizens Bank	$500	2.40%	Yes

(Continued)

Institution	Minimum Investment in a Five-year GIC	Interest Rate on a Five-year GIC	Insured by CDIC?
Chartered Banks			
Dundee Bank of Canada	$1,000	3.75%	Yes
HSBC Bank/Trust Canada	$1,000	2.60%	Yes
ICICI Bank Canada	$1,000	4.40%	Yes
ING Direct	$0	4.00%	Yes
Laurentian Bank	$1,000	2.60%	Yes
Manulife Bank	$2,500	3.60%	Yes
National Bank	$1,000	2.60%	Yes
Pacific & Western Bank	$1,000	3.50%	Yes
President's Choice Financial	$0	3.80%	No
ResMor Trust Company	$1,000	3.80%	Yes
Royal Bank	$1,000	2.20%	Yes
State Bank of India (Canada)	$2,000	3.75%	Yes
TD Canada Trust	$1,000	2.60%	Yes
Trust and Loan Companies			
Canadian Western Trust	$5,000	2.85%	Yes
Community Trust	$5,000	3.80%	Yes
Concentra Financial	$1,000	2.60%	Yes
Effort Trust	$5,000	3.25%	Yes
Equitable Trust	$5,000	3.90%	Yes
Home Trust Company	$5,000	3.80%	Yes
MCAN Mortgage Corp.	$5,000	2.85%	Yes
Montreal Trust	$1,000	2.60%	Yes
Other Financial Institutions			
Achieva Financial	$1,000	4.50%	No
COMTECH Credit Union	$15,000	3.99%	No
Desjardins Financial Security	$500	4.00%	No
DUCA Financial Services Credit Union	$1,000	3.80%	No
FirstOntario Credit Union	$1,000	2.65%	No
Italian Canadian Savings & Credit Union	$1,000	2.75%	No
Manulife Investments	$5,000	3.70%	No
Meridian Credit Union	$1,000	3.35%	No

Institution	Minimum Investment in a Five-year GIC	Interest Rate on a Five-year GIC	Insured by CDIC?
Other Financial Institutions			
Outlook Financial	$1,000	4.60%	No
Pace Savings & Credit Union	$1,000	2.60%	No
PARAMA Lithuanian Credit Union	$1,000	3.25%	No
PCCU Financial Credit Union	$1,000	3.45%	No
So-Use Credit Union	$1,000	3.45%	No
Standard Life	$1,000	3.25%	No
Transamerica Life	$1,000	3.20%	No
Virtual One Credit Union	$1,000	3.70%	No

You can see that the lowest rate is 2.2%, offered by Royal Bank, and the highest rate is 4.6%, offered by Outlook Financial, a Manitoba-based credit union.

That brings up an important point: credit union deposits are not guaranteed by the CDIC, they are guaranteed by provincially run organizations. Outlook Financial is covered by the Credit Union Deposit Guarantee Corporation of Manitoba (http://www.cudgc.com). Credit unions in Ontario are covered by an organization called the Deposit Insurance Corporation of Ontario (http://www.dico.com), an Ontario provincial agency established under the *Credit Unions and Caisses Populaires Act, 1994.*

I have nothing against credit unions—they provide a legitimate alternative to the standard banks—but assuming you'd like the security of knowing your savings are guaranteed by the federal government through the CDIC, look over the list for the maximum rate for a CDIC member. It's ICICI Bank Canada at 4.4%. Want the security of one of the best-known names in banking? Then there's ING Direct at 4.0%.

In this case, why would you choose a Royal Bank rate of 2.2% when you can literally double that rate elsewhere and still be covered by the CDIC?

GIC RATES OF THE FUTURE

There is uncertainty about the future returns the stock market will yield but there is also uncertainty about where interest rates will go. There is an important difference, though: interest rates cannot go below zero and the stock market most definitely can.

That's why the strategies in this book will focus on fixed-income products, namely GICs. We are in a period of the lowest interest rates in history. The governments have to keep interest rates low to stimulate the economy. How long will they stay this low? No one knows, but the likelihood is at least for the few years it probably will take for the economy to recover.

Throughout this book, I will focus on rates that are available now on the assumption that interest rates will remain low for an extended period of time. This goes with my conservative philosophy. I don't want you to base your retirement plans purely on hope. I'd like you to plan based on logic, and maybe get pleasantly surprised if future returns end up being higher.

For example, do you know what annual interest rate a five-year GIC was paying in 1980? It was 12.36%. The average five-year GIC annual interest rate over the period 1980–2000 was 9.04%. Maybe those rates will appear again, but it's best not to base a retirement strategy on that possibility.

3

BUY A HOME AND PAY OFF THE MORTGAGE

Would you rather have an RRSP (or RRIF) worth $400,000, or a house worth $400,000?

Assuming you could have only one or the other, the answer is easy from a simple financial point of view: you'd rather have the house, and I'll tell you why.

The reason is that the funds in the RRSP/RRIF are locked in. You can't spend an RRSP or RRIF. You have to withdraw the funds and report the amount on your income tax return and pay tax on it. If you withdrew all $400,000 at once, a lot of it would be in the highest tax bracket. You'd only get to keep the amount left after tax. In Ontario in 2009 that would be approximately only $232,000.

This is because you got a tax refund in the first place when you made the RRSP contributions over the years.

There are many more reasons why I'd rather have the house than an RRSP.

YA GOTTA LIVE SOMEWHERE

If you don't own a home, where are you going to live? You'd have to rent and that obviously costs money. It is cheaper than owning but it still will cost you money each and every month for the rest of your life.

GAINS IN VALUE ARE TAX-FREE

The increase in value in your principal residence is not taxed as it occurs, and the difference between what you paid for your home and what you sell it for—the capital gain—is not taxed when you sell. The increase in value of an RRSP/RRIF is taxed when you withdraw it and it's taxed as regular income.

This is an important point to think about. If you own stocks or equity mutual funds in an RRSP, the capital gain on their sale is not taxed at 50% of the gain. The whole amount goes into the account and is taxed as regular income upon withdrawal. This sounds like tax-inefficient investing, but warrants further study.

We'll delve more into this in a later chapter on alternatives to RRSPs.

SOURCE OF CASH

It's true that a house is not really a good source of ready cash. In other words, it's not a "liquid" investment. You can't sell a little piece of it if you need some money.

But it can be used as collateral on a loan. This usually results in a lower interest rate because the financial institution loaning you the money has some security—if you default, they can force a sale of your home to recover the money you owe them.

GREAT SOURCE OF RETIREMENT FUNDS

I have heard more than a few stories about retired people needing to live in a retirement or nursing home when they become unable to look after themselves. Selling the principal residence at that time can be an excellent source of tax-free funds. In many cases it's the only way they could pay for it, as there are simply not enough savings.

I often get asked about reverse mortgages for retired people who are cash-poor but house-rich. It sounds like a good idea. You get to keep the house, borrow the money against it, and the loan only has to get paid back when you sell the house or pass away.

To be honest, I have never known anyone that has used one. But the research I have done has indicated several problems. First of all, the interest rates are usually quite high. There are also fees involved and I have read newspaper articles about people losing their homes in certain circumstances even though it was promised that this couldn't happen. Also, the contracts are exceedingly complicated and long. It's a case of "buyer beware."

It would seem much simpler, cheaper and less risky to simply take out a secured loan using your house as collateral. But do this before you need the money. The banks are great at giving out umbrellas when it's sunny but not after the rain starts!

SHOULD I BUY A HOUSE?

If you don't already own a house you have a big decision to make. We'll discuss whether you can afford one next, but think about whether owning a home is right for you. If you like to move a lot, you may not wish to tie yourself down to one location.

If you are required to move, you'll have to consider the risk of rising and falling home prices. For example, if the company you work for has a habit of relocating you, it may not be worth the risk of getting burned with a badly timed sale. Some companies have stopped guaranteeing employees that they won't lose on selling a house because of relocation. It's just too costly for them. In that case, you may decide not to accept the risk of getting burned personally— remember point number one: avoid the potential for personal financial disasters.

You may also enjoy renting because you don't have to worry about repairs and maintenance. I have lived in a home for about twenty years and I can tell you there is always something that needs fixing. It may be the roof needing new shingles, the yard needs some landscaping, the deck needs repair or the walls need repainting. Not to mention the standard chores: cutting the grass, shovelling the driveway and doing the gardening (ewww!). Or the more expensive ones, like buying a new furnace, air conditioner or windows.

CAN I AFFORD A HOUSE?

After you decide you'd like the security and peace of mind that comes with owning a house, you'll need to determine whether or not you can afford one.

When you apply for a mortgage, lenders usually rely on two rules to determine how much you can afford to pay. They are the Gross Debt Service and Total Debt Service ratios.

Gross Debt Service Ratio (GDS)

This rule says that your monthly housing costs should not exceed 32% of your gross household monthly income. Your gross household monthly income is the salary (before deductions for income taxes, Canada Pension Plan [CPP] and Employment Insurance [EI]) of you and your spouse. If you are self-employed it is your gross sales less business expenses before deductions. You also include any other sources of income, like investments and other non-employment income.

Your monthly housing costs include the mortgage payments (principal plus interest), property taxes and heating expenses.

Total Debt Service Ratio (TDS)

This rule states that your total monthly debt load should not be more than 40% of your gross monthly income. Your monthly debt load includes mortgage payments and other debt payments, like for car loans, credit cards, lines of credit and student loans.

JUST HOW MUCH HOUSE CAN I AFFORD?

The maximum price you can afford depends on several factors, including your household income, the down payment amount and the interest rate on the mortgage.

The Canadian Mortgage and Housing Corporation (CMHC) provides a lot of very useful information for potential home buyers. To give you an idea of the maximum price you can afford based on the 32% gross debt service ratio, the organization provides the following table (rounded to the nearest $100) at http://www.cmhc-schl.gc .ca/en/co/buho/hostst/hostst_002.cfm. It assumes average tax and heating costs and a mortgage rate of 8%, so if you can get a lower rate you may be able to do better than these estimates:

CMHC Maximum Home Prices

Household Income	5% Down Payment	Maximum Home Price	10% Down Payment	Maximum Home Price	25% Down Payment	Maximum Home Price
$25,000	$3,000	$60,000	$6,300	$63,000	$18,900	$75,600
30,000	3,900	78,000	8,200	82,000	24,700	98,800
35,000	4,800	96,000	10,100	101,000	30,300	121,200
40,000	5,700	114,000	12,000	120,000	36,000	144,000
45,000	6,600	132,000	13,900	139,000	41,700	166,800
50,000	7,500	150,000	15,800	158,000	47,400	189,600
60,000	9,300	186,000	19,600	196,000	58,800	235,200
70,000	11,050	221,000	23,400	234,000	70,100	200,400
80,000	12,500	250,000	27,200	272,000	81,500	326,000
90,000	14,400	288,000	31,000	310,000	92,800	371,200
$100,000	$16,275	$325,500	$34,800	$348,000	$104,300	$417,200

SAVING FOR THE DOWN PAYMENT

This is the hardest part of realizing your dream of home ownership. Even for a 5% deposit, according to the above chart you'd need to save about 12% ($3,000/$25,000) to 16% ($16,275/$100,000) of your gross household income before taxes. This is not going to be easy, but if you don't do it you'll never own a home.

Of course there may be other sources, including a gift from a parent, but when you think about it, the process of trying to save for a down payment is a valuable lesson in itself. That's because home ownership is going to be more expensive than renting. That extra amount of money you are trying to save as you continue to rent will probably be needed after you buy the house. In other words, you'll be forced to live on less income, which will be the case after you buy a home.

Buying with Less Than 20% Down

Currently in Canada you can buy a home with less than a 20% down payment; in fact, as little as 5% is allowed. There is a catch, however: you'll have to buy mortgage loan insurance, also known as mortgage default insurance.

Mortgage loan insurance protects the lender—your bank—in case you default and can't pay your mortgage. You may pay for the insurance in a lump sum, or you usually can have it added to the mortgage and pay it over the term of the mortgage.

Be careful not to confuse it with mortgage life insurance, which would pay off the balance of the mortgage if the person who took out the mortgage were to die.

WARNING: Mortgage companies love selling mortgage life insurance!

Be careful of this trap. Some mortgage companies will try to talk you into buying their mortgage life insurance. It often looks like a small amount and they can easily add it to your mortgage payment. Check the fine print, though. In some cases they don't reduce the premium even though your mortgage principal balance is declining. In other words, if you sign up for a $300,000 mortgage, and over the years pay it down to, say, $150,000, you'd think the premiums would decline by about 50% because the mortgage life insurance would only cover the mortgage balance—$150,000 not $300,000 in this case. But that's not always the case.

It may be a better option just to make sure your regular life insurance policy has a sufficient death benefit to pay off the balance of your mortgage and provide for your dependents. By the way, make it a term insurance policy, not whole or universal life, as it's much cheaper and simpler.

Mortgage loan insurance is currently provided by two organizations:

1. **Canada Mortgage and Housing Corporation.** CMHC is Canada's national housing agency, established as a government-owned corporation in 1946 to address Canada's post-war housing shortage. http://www.cmhc-schl.gc.ca
2. **Genworth Financial Canada.** "The Homeownership Company" works with lenders, mortgage brokers, real estate agents and builders to make homeownership more affordable and accessible throughout Canada. http://www.genworth.ca

Most mortgage loan companies require borrowers to finance the down payment from their own resources, such as gifts from relatives, RRSPs or savings. For down payments between 5% and 10%, CMHC allows lenders to offer borrowers the option of using other sources, such as loans and lender incentives, but there is a premium to do this. Here are the CMHC charges.

CMHC Premiums

Financing Required	Premium % of Loan Amount
Up to and including 80%	1
Up to and including 85%	1.75
Up to and including 90%	2
Up to and including 95% :	
Traditional Down Payment	2.75
Non-Traditional Down Payment	2.9
Extended Amortization Surcharges:	
Greater than 25 years, up to and including 30 years	0.2
Greater than 30 years, up to and including 35 years	0.4

- So, for example, if you wanted to buy a home for $300,000 and had a 10% down payment ($30,000) and therefore needed to finance 90% ($270,000), the premium would be $5,400 (2% of $270,000).
- If you were able to come up with a down payment of 20% ($60,000) and therefore needed to finance only 80% ($240,000), the premium would only be $2,400 (1% of $240,000).

Note that mortgage loan insurance premiums in Ontario and Quebec are subject to provincial sales tax and the provincial sales tax cannot be added to the loan amount.

PRE-APPROVED MORTGAGES

It's a great idea to get pre-approval for a mortgage. This simply means that before you buy a house, you find a lending institution and get them to investigate your financial situation in order to give you a guaranteed mortgage up to a certain amount.

There is nothing more stressful financially than finding the house of your dreams and sitting on pins and needles wondering if your bank will approve your mortgage and allow you to move in. Trust me, I've been there.

Going through this step also can save an incredible amount of wasted time if your search takes you into a price range that you cannot afford.

If you are pre-approved, the lender will give you a written certificate indicating the amount, the interest rate and the length of time it is good for.

Remember to bring the following to the potential lender:

- personal identity confirmation, like a driver's licence
- details regarding your salary or self-employment earnings (latest T4 from employment, Notices of Assessment from Canada Revenue Agency)
- a listing of your net worth—your assets (bank accounts, RRSPs, cars, etc.) and your debts (lines of credit, credit cards, bank loans)
- amount of down payment you have and where it is coming from
- details as to how you'll pay the closing costs, including legal fees and the land transfer tax (this is often between 1.5% and 4% of the purchase price)

WHAT IF I DON'T QUALIFY?

Your calculations may indicate that you'll have problems getting approved for a mortgage based on your income and financial situation. The CMHC has the following suggestions:

- work first on paying down your existing debt
- wait to save a larger down payment
- look for a less expensive house
- meet with a credit counsellor who can help get your spending and debt under control
- buy your home through a rent-to-own program provided by the builder, a non-profit sponsor or a government sponsor
- find out about programs through which you can help build your own home
- ask the housing department of your municipality about any special programs available

One of the first things a potential lender will do to decide whether to loan you any money is to check your credit report. It's therefore vital that you know all about it.

Your Credit Report

Your credit report is a history of your credit activities that lenders obtain from a credit reporting agency commonly known as a credit bureau. Credit bureaus rely on information gathered from credit grantors (banks, credit card companies, retail stores, etc.) and public records (legal judgments, etc.) to make their determinations.

When you sign for a consumer loan, credit card, lease for a car, or line of credit, you are permitting the credit grantors to share the credit information with the appropriate credit reporting bureaus.

You have the right to see what's on your credit report and you should do this before you give a lender the right to ask for it so you can improve it if necessary and make any corrections that are required.

There are currently two credit bureaus in Canada. They are:

1. **Equifax Canada Inc.** Consumers may obtain a copy of their credit report, plus credit score and a score analysis online in Canada for a fee. They provide consumers online, real-time access to their credit information. Consumers provide personal information during the order process for their credit information so that their identity can be verified. http://www.equifax.ca

2. **TransUnion of Canada.** Consumers are asked to provide information that confirms their identity, plus valid credit card payment information, when applicable. Following a confirmation of their information, consumers may view their TransUnion Personal Credit Report & Score online. Ordering online is available to current or former residents of Canada. Fees may vary by province. http://www.transunion.ca

What's in a Credit Report

A credit report contains the basic identification information, including your name, address, date of birth, current employment information, as well as your Social Insurance Number. It usually doesn't include your credit score (usually your FICO score, which we will discuss soon), which you'll need to pay extra to obtain.

Here's what it does include:

- credit information reported by creditors to the reporting agency on existing debts
- overall comments on your historical credit performance
- any bankruptcy
- voluntary deposit—orderly payment of debt, credit counselling
- any registered consumer proposals
- judgments, seizure of movables/immovables, garnishment of wages
- secured loans (court name, date filed and creditor's name)
- collection accounts
- list of inquiries from creditors relating to credit applications you have made
- public court reports

Information reported by credit grantors often includes:

- phone number (of the credit grantor)
- account number
- type of account (revolving like a credit card or installment like a car lease)
- date opened
- months reviewed (how long you have had it)
- status (paid as agreed or not)
- payment history (if any minimum required payments have been late)
- credit limit
- payment amount (minimum payment for credit cards, monthly lease amounts of car leases)
- balance amount (how much was owing the last time the credit grantor reported)
- past due amount (if any)
- date of last activity
- date reported
- other comments (e.g., monthly payments)

How to Get a Free Copy of Your Credit Report

If you make a request in writing and mail or fax it to either of the credit bureaus, they will mail you a copy of your credit report free of charge.

Equifax also allows you to order one by phone by calling 1-800-465-7166. The automated telephone system will ask you to key in your Social Insurance Number (SIN), street number, apartment number (if applicable), postal code and a major credit card number if you have one. The organization says the report will then be mailed to your home address in about five days. I just ordered mine and it came as promised.

Getting Your Credit Report Online

If you'd like your credit report right away you can order it online from either of the credit bureaus *for a fee.*

For example, currently at Equifax for $23.95 you can get

- your FICO credit score
- your personalized credit report
- a full explanation of your score and how lenders view your credit risk
- tips on how you can improve your credit score
- custom graphs showing how you rank versus other Canadians
- specific factors that most affect your credit score

For $15.50 you can receive your credit report and tips about how to improve it, but you won't receive your FICO score.

WHAT IS A FICO CREDIT SCORE?
The FICO score was developed by Fair, Isaac and Company, often referred to as the pioneer of credit scoring. It's a number between 300 and 900 that lenders use to judge your credit risk. It is important to note that it's a snapshot of your credit risk at a point in time. Your score changes depending on your financial activities over time. The higher your credit score, the more likely you are to be approved for loans and to receive favourable interest rates when you are approved.

WHAT AFFECTS YOUR FICO CREDIT SCORE?

Your credit score is affected by many things but most important are the following:

- number of accounts not paid as agreed
- total credit balance related to total credit limits available
- whether credit lines revolve regularly or whether they remain fully utilized
- number of credit inquiries made in the last year by creditors
- existence of judgments, executions and writs in the public records

---

AN IMPORTANT WARNING:

You should be aware of one important thing about your credit rating. Even if you are well off and earn a good salary, your rating could be low. If you are not aware of this it could lead to major problems. Let me give you an example.

I know a woman who makes over $150,000 a year and has no credit card debt or any other debt for that matter. She also owns a house worth about $900,000 with a mortgage of less than half that. But you know what? Her credit rating is so low she could not even get a credit card. That's because the credit she and her family have are all in her husband's name. Her credit card is a secondary card of her husband's.

If her husband were to die, she would be left in a very difficult financial situation—unable to get credit of any kind. In her case she should apply for a basic card and begin using it to establish her credit rating.

How to Improve Your Credit Score

If your credit score needs improving, the most important steps you can take include

- **Pay your bills on time.** Pay them a day or so early if you can, because if they are even a day or two late it affects your score.
- **Pay down the balance.** The higher the balance and the closer you are to your credit limits, the lower your score.
- **Limit the amount of credit you apply for.** Each creditor makes an inquiry and excess inquiries reduce your rating.
- **Pay down lines of credit periodically.** Even if you have to draw them back up later, pay them down when you can to show positive activity.

- **Be careful with your credit cards.** Lost credit cards are a major source of credit problems. Check that you have them all from time to time and if you ever lose one, report it immediately to the credit card company. If you don't you could be on the hook for a lot of money that you did not spend.

YOUR HOME AS AN INVESTMENT

Remember we decided that we'd rather have a home worth $400,000 than an RRSP/RRIF worth the same amount? Well, there are other reasons besides the tax one. They include those ugly DSC fees to cash out your RRSP/RRIF if the investments were in mutual funds. What if your RRSP was worth $400,000 in June of 2008 and was invested substantially in equities? Poof. It's probably worth less than $300,000 now.

It's true a house can decline in value too and investing in a house because it appreciates in value is never a 100% guarantee, but consider this: if you don't own one you'll have to pay rent for the rest of your life.

Let's move on to another real-life story about the housing strategy.

"THE BEST INVESTMENT I EVER MADE"

In researching this chapter I asked a couple of individuals in the "seasoned" category—roughly eighty years old—what their best financial move was. Both immediately replied "my houses."

I found that a little surprising for several reasons. First of all, both individuals had spent their working years (the fifties to the nineties) in the prime bull years of the stock market—the post–World War II era— and invested predominantly in equities. One, whom I'll call Joe, even worked the majority of his career in the investment industry. Here's an investment professional who had daily access to financial information because it was his job, able to invest with little or no fees to drag him back, during the heyday of stocks, and his best move was his house-buying strategy. Interesting, eh?

Here's Joe's story:

In 1951, when I graduated from the University of Western Ontario, a friend's parents died and their house sold for

$8,000. I remember thinking at the time that not much changed from the value in the 1930s, but perhaps it was $3,000 then!

Jill and I moved to New York in 1962 and rented a one-bedroom flat in the centre of Manhattan on East 81st Street for $300 per month, which I remember was roughly twice the going rate for larger, two-bedroom flats in Toronto! I pleaded with my business partners in Toronto to subsidize me, to no avail. I was earning at the rate of $16,000 per annum. Not bad, as I later found out.

We moved to London, England, in 1968 and came back to Toronto in 1974—renting all that time. A centre-hall-plan house that I looked at on Douglas Drive in Rosedale in 1972 that was $50,000 had risen in value to over $100,000 in 1974. We had gone through rampant inflation at a rate of 12% plus in 1971 and it was still with us. By 1974 it didn't look like things were going to get cheaper so we bought a house for $174,000 (a one-hundred-year-old on South Drive), largely financed with a bank loan borrowed against my investment company shares (good as gold!). In 1972 we had received a 100% dividend, which made an enormous difference. It was not to happen again!

Inflation of house prices continued and we wanted to move, so we sold the house in 1978/9 for $309,000 and bought one (a converted bungalow in North Rosedale) for $264,000. I can thank my wife for that.

This is hard to believe, but we sold that house in 1987 for $779,000.

Many well-off people moved into this desirable area, partly because a senior Ontario politician bought a house around the corner from me on Douglas (one that looked very much like the one I looked at in 1972 for $50,000) for $1,000,000 *or very close to it. The house of my family lawyer's mother, a modest two-storey on Douglas was sold for $1,000,000 (right across the street from the politician's house) and one 300 feet from it was sold to another individual for $1,000,000. I said at the time, "I don't think we can afford to live here anymore," particularly as I had left the investment company and I was seriously thinking about, and subsequently did, resign from the other investment firm I had joined, because I thought that the U.S. owners were going to sewer the U.S. firm as well as the Canadian one. They did.*

So in 1987 we sold the Toronto house, and bought this house in Oakville for $439,000 and put the balance in the investment account. Not that it matters, but the new house is supposed to be in the $800,000 to $900,000 range now.

All boats rise in an up market, and historically, we have been in one for some fifty-odd years . . . rising at different rates over the years but nonetheless rising. Pressure of population increase drives it, certainly in the real estate market, but it always gets ahead of itself and corrects, sometimes for a very long time. The approximately 20% decline from 1987 to 1995 is a good example. We are in one of those periods now, I believe.

Let's summarize the gains Joe has realized since 1974. In 1978 his gain was $135,000, in 1987 he had a gain of $515,000 and in 2008 his unrealized gain was $361,000, assuming the low end of his value estimate. The total gain over the years? More than $1 million—$1,011,000, actually. And it was all tax free.

Obviously we have no idea if this trend will continue for the housing market, but when I compare it to the volatility of the stock market, personally I'd put my money in bricks and mortar.

CONCLUSION

You simply can't beat a house as an investment. Sure it may rise and fall in value but these fluctuations usually don't come close to the peaks and valleys of the stock market. In the long-term, it's usually the best investment anyone ever makes.

Combine that with the fact that the gain on sale is tax-free and you've got a winning combination that is tough to beat.

4

REDUCING EXPENSES DOESN'T HAVE TO BE PAINFUL

Almost everyone preaches at us to watch the small expenses. "Save the pennies and the dollars will look after themselves." Skip a coffee a day and you'll get rich. It's all a load of bunk. A few pennies or even dollars saved here and there won't add up to a hill of beans. And what's worse, those little things are what make life great: an intimate meal at a cozy restaurant, a steaming Tim Hortons caramel hot smoothee, a cherry float on a hot summer's day. There's got to be a better way than giving up life's treasures!

Why not focus your energy on reducing what are probably two of your largest expenses, while not sacrificing anything? You can, and it's easy.

Those expenses are interest and taxes.

REDUCING INTEREST

Unfortunately, as soon as we move out of our parents' house life starts to get expensive. We may want to go to university and that brings tuition fees, food, lodging and entertainment expenses. Often, people have to go into debt via student loans simply to afford the education.

Next may come some travelling—say, to Europe. OK, that's going to cost you. Add it to the student debt.

Want to get married? Add the expenses for things like the ring, the honeymoon . . .

Want to live somewhere? You'll probably need a mortgage to pay for your dream home.

Maybe some kids would be good to have around. Do yourself a favour: don't do a cash flow projection to determine if you're going to reproduce or not. They're a big cash outflow!

The result? In our late twenties or early thirties (usually) we end up with a mortgage, possibly a line of credit, a car loan and maybe some credit card debt. And that's assuming we've paid off the student loan.

All that debt means we pay a lot of interest each and every year. It simply makes sense to focus on minimizing our interest expenses because it is often one of our biggest cash drains. I call the years between moving out on our own until the debts are all paid off "the Spending Years."

THE SPENDING YEARS

Reducing interest expenses during the Spending Years is the key to getting ahead. There are two ways to reduce the interest you pay:

1. Reduce the amount of the debt.
2. Reduce the interest rate on the debt.

To reduce the interest rate, for example, if you are in credit card debt paying punishing interest of 20% or more a year, simply changing to a basic no frills card at prime plus a percent or two could save you thousands of dollars a year.

But let's start with the more significant one—reducing the amount of debt itself.

Reducing the Amount of the Debt

Obviously, the more debt we have, the greater the amount of interest we'll have to pay on that debt. Reducing the principal amount of the debt should be your number one goal.

During the Spending Years this is going to be difficult. There are many demands for money and deciding to cut back on one area or another will probably be hard, but it is the most important step to gaining control of your finances and setting yourself up for a comfortable retirement.

The first step to achieving this goal of reducing debt is to know what your debt balance is. Do you even know? Do yourself a favour and figure it out right now.

Go and get last month's statements for your mortgage, car loan, line of credit and any credit cards, as well as any other debts you might have. List all these debts in the first column. Then, list the principal balance of each in the second column, the total payment you made last month in the third, the interest portion of that payment in the fourth, the interest you'll pay in the next year in the fifth, the years left on the loan in the sixth and the interest rate in the seventh.

The interest you'll pay in the next year will probably be the hardest to calculate unless you have a payment schedule from your bank or finance company for any fixed-term loans like mortgages and car loans. This "amortization schedule" should show the principal balance and the principal and interest portion of each payment. For variable rate loans with open terms, simply multiply the average balance of the loan times the interest rate. For many people this will be a real eye-opener because they simply haven't ever done it before—they don't know how much debt they are in.

Let's try doing it for someone we'll call Jimmy. Here's his chart:

Type of Debt	Principal Balance	Total Payment Last Month	Interest Paid Last Month	Interest Paid Annually	Years Left on Loan	Interest Rate
Five-year Mortgage	$150,000	$1,075	$750	$8,891	20	6%
Car Loan	$15,000	$366	$100	$1,080	4	8%
Line of Credit	$10,000	$200	$63	$750	5	7.5%
Credit Card (Gold)	$11,000	$291	$183	$2,200	5	20%
Total	$186,000	$1,932	$1,096	$12,921		

The first thing to notice about Jimmy is that he's been spending more than he makes. He has $10,000 on an unsecured line of credit charging 7.5% a year and $11,000 on a credit card at 20% interest. If Jimmy continues to spend more than he makes, his plans for a nice retirement are in jeopardy.

Just look at what his debt is costing him. The interest paid annually on his line of credit and credit card is $2,950 ($750 on the line of credit and $2,200 on the credit card). That's almost $3,000 down the toilet each year.

How long before he'll have the line of credit and credit card paid off? Five years. So he'll end up wasting about $15,000 in interest if he continues his current habits.

But here's the real problem: His current debt will take five years to pay off *if he doesn't add anything else to it.*

The real problem most people have, Jimmy included, is that their lifestyles demand that they keep spending as they have in the past. For example, Jimmy could pay down his credit card by $1,000 one month, but if he can't resist putting that big screen TV on it for $1,500, he'll end up worse off by $500 plus the additional interest.

I know that sounds simple, and it is—it's a simple concept— but changing your lifestyle will be tough for anyone that has debt balances.

Debt and the Economy

But when you think about it, what we have just talked about is cause for very real concern these days. If many consumers have been spending more than they make, buying goods and services they can't afford, and this keeps the economy humming, what happens when they hit their breaking point? What happens when they can't borrow any more because their debt levels are maxed out?

Isn't that what just happened in the U.S. in the fall of 2008? The consequences have been very ugly. Companies started to report huge losses as sales dove, with hundreds of thousands of job losses as a result. People couldn't make their payments and mortgages and loans defaulted at a record pace. Many people were forced to sell their homes at fire-sale rates as house prices plummeted.

What's worse is that the problem was not contained within the U.S. It seems people worldwide followed the same debt-acquiring strategy—they wanted the good life, too.

How are they trying to fix the problem? The U.S. and other governments worldwide are pumping more money into the system by basically printing it, loaning it to the banks and asking them to loan it to consumers. Well, I guess that's all they can do, but it sounds too easy to me.

Isn't the real problem that in much of U.S. industry costs are too high and demand for the goods is low? Shouldn't the focus be on the businesses starting to work more efficiently, producing what the consumers want, rather than governments bailing them out with cash infusions and trying to force banks to loan people money to continue to spend more than they make buying things they don't need?

The governments can play economic games like printing more money, reducing interest rates to encourage people to spend when they are already spending more than they make, and bailing out companies by investing in them, but ultimately will this do anything other than delay the inevitable? It's like putting a bandage on a severely broken leg. It may help but it doesn't solve the basic problem—the leg is still broken.

Put another way, trying to keep a bubble from bursting by pumping more air into it will result in a big bang sooner or later.

Reducing the Interest Rate on the Debt

OK, I think you get my drift. Let's get back to you and your situation. You want to reduce the interest you pay on your debt.

The most important thing you can do is make sure your credit rating is as high as possible. The better it is, the easier it will be for you to shop around for the best interest rate, because lenders will be bidding against each other for your business. That puts you in the driver's seat.

The other thing you can do to reduce the interest you pay on the debt you do have, is to restructure it.

Let's take Jimmy, for example. The first thing he should do is rank his debt from highest interest rate to lowest. The credit card debt comes out on top at 20%. He should reduce his payments on any lower interest debt that he can and apply the excess to the credit card debt.

But interestingly, here is where the financial institutions have the advantage. He simply can't reduce his mortgage payments—the debt with the lowest interest rate. Jimmy happens to be locked in for the next five years. He has no choice but to continue to make the payments each and every month on his mortgage while the bank lets him pay down as little as 3% a month on his high-interest credit card. Gee, thanks!

He can, however, reduce the payments on his line of credit at 7.5% to the lowest amount possible and increase the amount he pays on his credit card. He should also call his bank and at least several other credit card issuers to replace his gold card with a more basic one. Competitors will often offer a low rate or balance transfer.

WARNING: The following strategy *could* be dangerous to your financial health!

Ever heard of "debt consolidation"? It's the process of taking your existing debt and combining it into one loan at a lower interest rate.

Jimmy could apply to see if he could combine his line of credit and credit card debt into one loan, possibly secured by his house, to reduce the interest rate.

U.S. consumers, however, have provided us with a glimpse of how this strategy can be a financial killer. Many borrowed up to the limit on the value of their home, continued to spend more than they made and ran up their credit cards and lines of credit again. Then the housing market declined and they were left with a mortgage worth more than their home, as well as other debt. This is a personal financial disaster of epic proportions.

GET THREE QUOTES
Well-run businesses always get at least a few quotes for large purchases of goods or services. Why should you be any different? Call at least three different financial institutions when it comes time to renew your mortgage, line of credit, etc. This will ensure that the competitive bid process is used to get the best rate available.

REDUCING TAXES

Nobody likes to pay taxes, and reducing them should be on everyone's mind. What could be less painful than a simple switch of two numbers on you and your spouse's tax returns that reduces the taxes you pay by a thousand dollars?

That's one reason I recommend that you pay to have a professional prepare your income tax returns. If you don't and you miss certain opportunities it could cost you dearly. I also recommend that you pay a professional to make a detailed analysis of your family's tax situation with an eye to reducing taxes. This is obviously more beneficial if your financial life is at all complicated. You may find it money very well spent.

Because this book is 100% Canadian, we can focus on the major simple tax strategies that will save you money. I am not taking about complex trust structures or offshore investing. Just basic moves that many Canadians don't know about or aren't taking advantage of.

Pension Income Splitting

The new pension income-splitting rules could save you thousands of dollars in tax every year—painlessly. Let's discuss how the rules work.

For 2007 and later taxation years, you are allowed to transfer up to 50% of your "eligible pension income" to your spouse or common-law partner.

Income that qualifies for pension splitting depends on the recipient's age. Here's what qualifies depending on how old you are.

For recipients under age sixty-five:

- pension income from a registered pension plan (RPP), for example, pensions from an employer-sponsored defined benefit (DB) or defined contribution (DC) plan
- certain other payments received as a result of the death of a spouse or common-law partner (e.g., a survivor pension annuity)

For recipients age sixty-five and older:

- both payments described above
- annuity payments from an RRSP

- RRIF withdrawals or withdrawals from RRIFs subject to federal or provincial locked-in legislation, such as Life Income Funds (LIFs) and LRIFs
- annuity payments received from a deferred profit sharing plan (DPSP)

Also note that eligible pension income amounts also qualify for the $2,000 pension income non-refundable tax credit.

In other words, if you are sixty-five years of age and older, all your pension income is eligible for the transfer. If you are not sixty-five at the end of the year, only your income eligible for the pension income credit is eligible for pension splitting.

The reason that the government limits the requirements for RRSP annuity, RRIF and LRIF income to those age sixty-five and over is to target pension splitting and the pension income credit to retired people.

You have much less control over the timing of registered pension plan payments than you do over the amount and timing of withdrawals under RRSPs, RRIFs and LRIFs. Without the age sixty-five rule, people who aren't retired could gain tax advantages through income splitting well before age sixty-five. Pensioners who receive RPP income generally have little say in the timing of their pension payments, since they usually only begin to receive payments after they retire.

What You Can't Split

Note that pension income for splitting purposes does not include Old Age Security (OAS) benefits, CPP or QPP benefits, death benefits, retiring allowances, RRSP withdrawals (other than annuity payments), or payments out of a Retirement Compensation Arrangement (RCA), salary deferral arrangement or employee benefit plan.

A foreign pension annuity may qualify for income splitting, but not the portion that is tax exempt because of a tax treaty with the foreign country. Income from a U.S. Individual Retirement Account (IRA) also does not qualify.

How to Split Pension Income

To split your pension income, both you and your spouse or common-law partner will have to make a joint election by completing form

T1032—Joint Election to Split Pension Income. You'll need to file the form with the tax return for the year the pension income is being split. For example, for the 2009 tax year you'll need to file it by April 30, 2010 or, if you're self-employed, by June 15, 2010.

If income tax has been withheld from the pension income, remember to allocate the tax withheld in the same ratio that you reported the pension income.

You have to make the pension income-splitting election on an annual basis. In other words, your decision for 2009 will not carry forward automatically. Each year you'll need to decide how much of your eligible pension income (if any) you want to split.

To be eligible, you and your spouse or common-law partner must be living together and residents of Canada at the end of the year or at the date of death of one of you if that happened during the year.

If you and your spouse or common-law partner are living separately at the end of the year due to a breakdown of the relationship, which has lasted for at least ninety days, no transfer is permitted.

If you married or commenced living common-law during the year or if your spouse or common-law partner died during the year, you must pro-rate the amount eligible for transfer by the number of months the relationship existed. The month the relationship began or your spouse or common-law partner died counts as a full month. The number of months the relationship existed is divided by twelve to get the amount you can transfer.

There are two main benefits to splitting pension income.

Advantage #1: Less Tax

As you know, if the transferee spouse or common-law partner is in a lower marginal tax bracket at the time of the transfer, as a couple your combined tax will be lower. That's because the taxable income of the higher tax bracket spouse will be decreased and the taxable income of the lower tax bracket spouse will be increased.

If you are doing your own calculations to optimize the transfer, the benefits of using a computer-based program speak for themselves, unless you like doing dozens of manual calculations!

Advantage #2: The $2,000 Pension Credit

If the transferee spouse is sixty-five or over at the end of the taxation year for which you are splitting pension income, the transferee may include the transferred income along with any other eligible pension income in claiming the $2,000 pension income credit.

Therefore, if your spouse or common-law partner is not already eligible to utilize his or her $2,000 pension credit, he or she will be able to reduce the tax bill. This may result in a combined credit of $4,000 instead of $2,000 as you both make the claim.

If the transferee spouse or common-law partner is not yet sixty-five at the end of the tax year, he or she may still claim the amount of qualified pension income that is transferred. In this case, the eligible pension income would include the transferor's private pension or annuity income plus certain amounts received as a result of the death of his or her former spouse or common-law partner. Note that in this situation the transferor's RRSP, RRIF or DPSP income does not qualify.

Advantage #3: Increasing OAS Benefits

Depending on your current net income levels, diverting pension income to your spouse or common-law partner could increase your OAS benefit by reducing the amount of the OAS clawback.

The maximum OAS benefit for 2009 is $6,203, but it is reduced (or clawed back) by 15% of net income in excess of $66,335. The entire amount of OAS is clawed back when your net income reaches $107,692, because 15% of $107,692 less $66,335 equals $6,203, the whole OAS pension.

So if your net income exceeds $66,335 in 2009 and you can reduce your net income by allocating some of your pension income to your spouse or common-law partner, you might reduce the amount of OAS that would otherwise have been clawed back when you filed your 2009 tax return. It should be noted that if the splitting results in your spouse or common-law partner's net income being above $66,335, his or her OAS benefit may be reduced.

Advantage #4: Increasing Other Credits

It is important to note that it is possible for a low income spouse or common-law partner to transfer unused non-refundable tax credits including age, pension, child and tuition/education/textbook amounts to his or her higher income spouse or common-law partner. To the extent that the lower-income spouse had other non-refundable and non-transferrable amounts eligible that can be used to offset the transferred pension income, there would be a net tax savings.

Also, the transferor may be able to increase some other non-refundable credits like the age amount, which would have been reduced by his or her higher income before the transfer.

How Much Pension Income Should You Transfer?

If you and your spouse or common-law partner are in the same income tax bracket and are both using the full $2,000 pension non-refundable tax credit, there is probably no benefit to transferring any pension income.

If, however, one of you is in a higher income tax bracket, it's probably best to transfer an amount to bring your spouse or common-law partner up to the amount of income where your tax bracket starts. If he or she is in an even lower tax bracket, the maximum 50% is probably the answer.

Even if you are both in the same income tax bracket, it probably makes sense to transfer at least enough pension income so your spouse or common-law partner can fully utilize the $2,000 pension credit, assuming the pension income transferred is eligible for credit in his or her hands if he or she is under sixty-five.

How to Make the Pension Income Transfer

You and your spouse or common-law partner must each fill in the line 314 federal worksheet that comes with the T1 income tax package, but the actual election is then made on form T1032. The transferor deducts the transfer amount on line 210 of his or her income tax return and the transferee spouse or common-law partner adds the same amount to his or her income on line 116 of his or her return. Form T1032 will show you how much pension credit each of you can claim on line 314.

Spousal RRSPs: Still a Useful Tool

With the new rules allowing you to split RRSP annuity and RRIF income, are spousal RRSPs still useful? In a word, yes.

A spousal (or common-law partner) RRSP is a plan in which one spouse or common-law partner has contributed to an RRSP and the other spouse or common-law partner is the owner or annuitant. It is often used by couples for post-retirement income-splitting purposes, as funds are withdrawn and taxed in the hands of the annuitant spouse rather than the contributor spouse. If the annuitant spouse is in a lower tax bracket than the contributor spouse at the time of the withdrawal, there can be a reduction of the couple's tax bill.

The amount you can contribute to a spousal RRSP is determined by the contributor's RRSP limits, not the annuitant's. In other words, it doesn't matter if your spouse or common-law partner does not work and therefore has no RRSP room—it's your room that counts.

Contributions to a spousal plan become the property of your spouse or common-law partner; however, there is one important catch to be aware of. If funds are withdrawn within three taxation years of *any* contribution to the plan, the withdrawal will be reportable by the contributor spouse or partner, effectively ruining the strategy.

Advantage #1: Splitting Income Under Age Sixty-Five

Under the pension-splitting rules, if you are under sixty-five, eligible pension income includes only payments from an RPP, and generally not amounts paid from an RRSP or RRIF. Therefore, anyone who wishes to retire before age sixty-five who does not have an RPP should still consider the use of a spousal RRSP to allow the withdrawals to be taxed in a lower income spouse or common-law partner's hands without having to wait until age sixty-five.

If you have determined that you don't need the maximum you could put into an RRSP to fund your retirement, there is another way to split income well before retirement. A high-income spouse could make spousal RRSP contributions and get the tax refund at the high marginal tax rate. After waiting the required three years, the spouse or common-law partner could withdraw the amount and pay the lower amount of tax. This essentially shifts income from a high bracket to a low bracket over three-year intervals.

Advantage #2: Splitting More Than 50%

It may make sense for a couple to transfer more than the 50% allowed under the pension-splitting rules. For example, a very high-income person with a spouse or common-law partner who does not work may wish to transfer up to 100% of his or her RRSP to the non-working spouse or common-law partner.

This is possible with a spousal RRSP but not regular pension splitting.

Advantage #3: Contributions Past Age Seventy-one

When you turn seventy-one, you'll convert your RRSP to a RRIF as required. You can, however, continue to contribute to a spousal RRSP if you have RRSP contribution room and your spouse or common-law partner is under age seventy-two.

In fact, if you continue working into your seventies, you may still be generating "earned income" for RRSP purposes and thus be able to contribute to a spousal RRSP as long as your spouse or common-law partner is under age seventy-two.

It should also be noted that even if you aren't working but own a rental property, net rental income from a rental property also qualifies as earned income for purposes of calculating eligible RRSP contribution room.

Advantage #4: Home Buyers' Plan Withdrawals

An RRSP Home Buyers' Plan (HBP) allows new home buyers to withdraw up to $25,000 from their RRSPs for the down payment on a new home. This allows people with no other savings than their RRSPs to get into a home.

If one spouse is working and the other is not, the working spouse could contribute $25,000 to his or her own RRSP and $25,000 to a spousal RRSP over the years, allowing $25,000 each or $50,000 to be withdrawn under the HBP.

Advantage #5: RRSP Deduction Upon Death

If an individual dies with unused RRSP contribution room available, the executor of the deceased's will can make an RRSP contribution to a surviving spouse or common-law partner's spousal RRSP and get an RRSP deduction on the deceased's final tax return.

How to Calculate Your Tax Bill

Why wait until April of the next year to find out how much tax you owe or what refund you'll get for the prior year? Most people do just that—wait until the tax preparer has completed their tax return to give them the good or bad news about their refund or balance owing. That's a mistake. The sooner you start thinking about your tax bill, the more likely it is that you will be able to make adjustments to save you tax.

You can also get a jump on maximizing the tax benefits of using pension income splitting.

It's easy to do your own calculations at any time using a free tool on a Canada Revenue Agency (CRA) website. The advantage to this is that it's easy to play with the figures to see the effect of any of the strategies we've talked about.

Try it now. Google "Payroll Deductions Online Calculator" or go to http://www.cra-arc.gc.ca/esrvc-srvce/tx/bsnss/pdoc-eng.html.

The program operates on the website, so there's no need to download it to your computer and worry about whether it will work on your operating system. It calculates payroll deductions for all provinces (except for Quebec) and territories based on information you provide. To perform calculations for Quebec you'll need to download the WinRAS program from Revenu Québec (google "WinRAS Revenu Quebec") or go to http://www.revenu.gouv.qc.ca/eng/services/sgp_winras/.

It is important to note that the Payroll Deductions Online Calculator program applies the exact salary amount to determine the tax deductions. The Tables on Diskette, including the printed publications "Payroll Deductions Tables" and "Payroll Deductions Supplementary Tables," apply the mid-point of the salary range to determine the tax deductions. Both methods result in tax deduction amounts that may be slightly different, but both are acceptable to the CRA.

All you have to do is enter the following information:

- the period of the required salary or commission calculation (usually the January to June or July to December period,

as the government usually updates the tables as of July 1)
- province or territory of employment
- the number of pay periods in the year, as follows:
  - daily (240 pay periods a year)
  - weekly (52 pay periods a year)
  - biweekly (26 pay periods a year)
  - semi-monthly (24 pay periods a year)
  - monthly (12 pay periods a year)
  - 10 pay periods a year
  - 13 pay periods a year
  - 22 pay periods a year
  - weekly (53 pay periods a year)
  - biweekly (27 pay periods a year)

You can also enter the employer's name and the pay period ending date, but these are optional fields.

If you know your gross salary and the amount of any taxable benefits you are receiving, you should be able to duplicate your pay stub details from your employer.

It can also reveal some interesting things about your tax situation.

Happy New Year—
Here's Your Reduced Paycheque

Ever wonder why your net pay seems to decline at the beginning of a new calendar year, even though you may have received a raise? That's because you again have to start making CPP and EI payments. In other words, as soon as your gross salary exceeds the CPP and EI limits ($46,300 and $42,300, respectively, for 2009) in a calendar year you will have had the maximum CPP and EI amount already withheld for that year. All your paycheques past that point will not have any CPP or EI withheld. The withholdings for the new year start with the first paycheque dated in the new year.

Let's look at an example. Say that you earned an annual gross salary of $80,000, including any taxable benefits in Ontario in 2009, and that you get paid monthly. In this case, in the CRA's program, select January 1, 2009 as the period of the required salary calculation, Ontario as the province and monthly pay periods, then click on the "Salary/Bonus/Retroactive Pay/Pension calculation" bar and you'll be taken to the next screen.

Click on "Determine gross income" and enter the amount of the monthly gross salary—$6,666.67 in this case ($80,000/12)—under income type "Salary or wages" without the dollar sign or comma, then click OK. You'll be taken back to the page where you can enter other items, including CPP and EI amounts deducted year-to-date, as well as federal and provincial claim code amounts (the total non-refundable tax credits you'll be claiming for the year). We'll assume it's the first paycheque of the year and therefore no CPP or EI has been withheld yet and only the basic personal exemption (Claim Code 1) applies federally and provincially.

Here's what the program comes up with when we click "Calculate":

Payroll Deductions Online Calculator Results—Effective January 1, 2009	
Employee's name	
Employer's name	
Pay period	Monthly (12 pay periods a year)
Pay period ending date	
Province of employment	Ontario
Federal amount from TD1	Claim Code 1 (Minimum - 10,100.00)
Provincial amount from TD1	Claim Code 1 (Minimum - 8,881.00)
Salary or wages for the pay period	6,666.67
Total EI insurable earnings for the pay period	6,666.67
Taxable income	6,666.67
Cash income for the pay period	6,666.67
Federal tax deductions	1,072.99
Provincial tax deductions	557.70
Requested additional tax deduction	0.00
Total tax on income	1,630.69
CPP deductions	315.56
EI deductions	115.33
Amounts deducted at source	0.00
Total deductions on income	2,061.58
Net amount	4,605.09

As you can see, your net pay would have been $4,605.09 after deductions of $315.56 for CPP and $115.33 for EI. After July your gross salary to date will have exceeded the CPP and EI maximums, so from the months of August to December 2009 your net pay will increase to $5,035.98 (gross of $6,666.67 less total taxes of $1,630.69).

The real benefit of this program, however, is that it also allows you to calculate your tax figures for an entire year. I find the easiest way to do this is to enter $0.01 as your gross income and enter your entire salary as a bonus.

In the example we have just looked at, if we enter $0.01 as the monthly salary and $80,000 as the bonus, here's what we get:

Payroll Deductions Online Calculator Results—Effective January 1, 2009	
Pay period	Monthly (12 pay periods a year)
Pay period ending date	
Province of employment	Ontario
Federal amount from TD1	Claim Code 1 (Minimum - 10,100.00)
Provincial amount from TD1	Claim Code 1 (Minimum - 8,881.00)
Salary or wages for the pay period	0.01
Total EI insurable earnings for the pay period	42,300.00
Taxable income	0.01
Cash income for the pay period	0.01
Federal tax deductions	0.00
Provincial tax deductions	0.00
Requested additional tax deduction	0.00
Total tax on income	0.00
CPP deductions	0.00
EI deductions	0.00
Amounts deducted at source	0.00
Total deductions on income	0.00
Total current bonus payable	80,000.00
Federal tax deductions on bonus	12,875.87
Provincial tax deductions on bonus	6,692.44
Total tax deductions on bonus	19,568.31
CPP deductions on bonus	2,118.60
EI deductions on bonus	731.79
RRSP, etc., deducted from current bonus	0.00
Total deductions on bonus	22,418.70
Total deductions on salary income and bonus	22,418.70
Net amount	57,581.31

There's your answer—$19,568.31 tax, $2,118.60 CPP and $731.79 EI for a net pay of $57,581.31.

Now the interesting part. What if you get a $10,000 bonus? Simply change the bonus from $80,000 to $90,000 and you'll find out your tax bill will increase to $23,909.27, resulting in net pay of $63,240.35 (CPP and EI deductions remain the same since they are already at the maximum). Your taxes rose by $4,340.96.

Marginal Tax Rates

We often hear the term "marginal tax rate" with respect to taxes and it's vital that you know exactly what that is. It is the additional amount of tax you would pay on an additional amount of income given your current income level. Basically it gets higher as your taxable income gets higher.

In the example we have been looking at, your marginal tax rate was 43.41% because you owed an additional $4,340.96 on an addition of $10,000 of taxable income.

The program will show that the $30,000 employee who gets an increase to $40,000 will owe an additional $2,294.39 in tax—that's a marginal tax rate of 22.94% ($2,294.39/$10,000).

But wait just one minute. This employee will also owe $495 more in CPP and $173 more in EI deductions, so the total tax/CPP/EI bill goes from $6,024.76 (tax of $4,020.76, CPP of $1,485 and EI of $519) to $8,987.15 (tax of $6,315.15, CPP of $1,980 and EI of $692). That is a total increase of $2,962.39— almost 30%. While not part of the marginal tax rate, the CPP and EI effect of salary increases on lower-income individuals can be significant.

Marginal tax rates are a powerful thing and the main key to getting your family's total tax bill under control. The following chart will help me explain how important this concept can be to reducing the taxes you pay. It shows the combined federal and Ontario income tax rates for 2008 assuming only the basic personal exemption:

Lower Limit	Upper Limit	Basic Tax	Rate on Excess
$0	$9,600	$0	0.00%
9,601	12,003	0	15.00%
12,004	15,326	360	27.10%
15,327	36,020	1,261	21.05%
36,021	37,885	5,617	24.15%
37,886	63,430	6,067	31.15%
63,431	72,041	14,025	32.98%
72,042	74,721	16,865	35.39%
74,722	75,769	17,813	39.41%
75,770	123,184	18,226	43.41%
$123,185		$38,809	46.41%

Note: the tax rates reflect budget proposals and news releases to March 19, 2008.

Look at the difference in the marginal tax rate or "rate on excess." For someone in the highest bracket (earning more than $123,185 a year) it's 46.41%. That means that if this person got a bonus of $10,000, $4,641 would go to the tax person and only $5,359 would be left.

For someone who has no other income, the first $9,600 ($10,100 in 2009) is tax free because that's the amount of the basic personal exemption—their marginal tax rate up to that amount is zero. If, for example, a couple with one in the highest bracket and the other in the lowest, could shift $10,000 in income from the higher to the lower, they would save $4,641 in tax. That's what's called "income splitting" and it's the key to saving taxes.

Self-Employment—
King of the Income Splitters

The problem with standard employment is that you don't have the flexibility to decide whose tax return the income goes on. You do the work, you get paid, your T4 employment slip comes in your name and you pay tax on the income.

The senior executive can't simply call the payroll department and say, "Can you please put $10,000 of my income on a separate T4 for my spouse?"

Want to save tax? Self-employment is worth a detailed look.

The reason for this is that you are allowed to pay reasonable salaries to a spouse as well as children who contribute to your business.

Let's take a look at an example. How much further ahead would a couple in their own business be compared to an executive that made the same amount of money?

Let's assume the executive had a gross salary of $130,000 in Ontario in 2008. Here's what his tax return would show:

One Executive

Gross Income	$130,000
Federal Income Tax	$25,016.43
Ontario Income Tax	$14,961.51
Total Taxes	$39,977.94
CPP Deduction	$2,049.30
EI Deduction	$711.03
Total Taxes, CPP and EI	$42,738.27
Net Amount	$87,261.73

Note that I have assumed non-refundable tax claims of $19,200 federally and $16,052 for Ontario to incorporate the claim for a spouse with no income.

If the executive was instead self-employed and could split the income with the spouse and report $90,000 and $40,000 on separate income tax returns, this is the result:

Self-Employment

	Spouse 1	Spouse 2	Combined
Gross Income	$90,000	$40,000	$130,000
Federal Income Tax	$15,283.96	$3,848.57	$19,132.53
Ontario Income Tax	$8,325.73	$2,148.54	$10,474.27
Total Taxes	$23,609.69	$5,997.11	$29,606.80
CPP Deduction	$2,049.30	$1,980.00	$4,029.30
CPP Deduction (self-employed)	$2,049.30	$1,980.00	$4,029.30
EI Deduction	$0	$0	
Total Taxes, CPP and EI	$27,708.29	$9,957.11	$37,665.40
Net Amount	$62,291.71	$30,042.89	$92,334.60

Note that the combined tax declines to $29,606.80 from $39,977.94. That's a significant savings of $10,371.14.

But, as with most things in personal finances, there are a few more issues that need to be hashed out.

First of all, when you are self-employed you don't have to pay into the EI system. The flip side of that coin is that if you go out of business you do not get to claim EI benefits.

CPP is a different story. Self-employed people have to make CPP contributions and, since there is no employer, they also have to pay the amount that the employer otherwise would have. That doubles the amount that each of the spouses have to pay. One of the amounts is claimed as a non-refundable tax credit and the other can be deducted from the self-employed person's taxable income. These CPP deductions have been taken into account in the table above.

Now don't take that as advice to quit your high-paying job because you don't like the tax bill—that would be nuts. Take it under consideration for the future. Self-employment income is easier to split than salary. If it makes sense in your case, you should consider it seriously.

But I Don't Know
Anything About Being Self-Employed

Well, maybe not, but given the financial environment we have just entered, you may be wise to start educating yourself about self-employment.

Think about it. Companies worldwide are being forced to cut costs any way they can. Mergers and acquisitions, government buyouts, or layoffs are being discussed in the majority of boardrooms at this very moment. Face it: there is no more job security. Jobs for life are a thing of the past.

All is not lost, however. Companies still need people to do the work even after layoffs. Going back into the workforce as a consultant is going to be a more and more common theme in the years to come.

Unfortunately, many people are going to be forced into this against their will. Think of a fifty-eight-year-old senior manager forced to retire from a company he has been with for thirty years. Where is he going to find a job in his field? He will be at a high pay level and there will be much younger/cheaper alternatives available to the companies he would be applying for a job at.

On the other hand, he would have plenty of experience and if he were to seek contract assignments he would be a lot cheaper than a full-time employee because of the cost of benefits. That's key to your pitch to a potential client: they won't have to pay for all your benefits like CPP, EI, Employer Health Tax, pensions, a health plan, Workers' Compensation, as well as potential severance payments.

Self-Employment Can Be Pretty Simple

Many people are scared of self-employment but you don't have to be. At its simplest form it can be one person operating out of his or her home. Here are some basic facts that should help to put your mind at ease:

- **The Name.** If you operate under your own name, e.g., Jane Smith, Consultant, you don't even need to register the business name. Just put that at the top of your letterhead and you are set to go.
- **Goods and Services Tax (GST).** Until you bill more than $30,000 in a single year you don't need to register for or start collecting the GST.
- **Bank Account.** If you operate under your own name you can make deposits to a personal bank account in your name. No need to open up a business account with higher bank fees.
- **Bookkeeping.** Don't worry about a fancy bookkeeping package at first. Just keep track of every expense related to your business so you can deduct them from your income.

CONCLUSION

There you have it—the information and tools you'll need to painlessly reduce two of the biggest expenses you'll probably ever have—interest and taxes.

Now let's delve into the next area—why it's best not to even consider starting your RRSP until later in life.

FORGET RRSPs UNTIL YOUR DEBT IS PAID OFF (THE OPPORTUNITY ZONE)

Yes, that's what I said, and yes, it goes against traditional retirement planning advice. You know, the "start early—the earlier the better" and "pay yourself first" type of advice. The truth is that it is really better to start late.

When you work through the numbers and consider the risks involved with investing in the stock market while you are still in debt, you may come to the same conclusion as I have: you are much better off to focus on buying a home and paying off all debt, including the home mortgage, before even starting to save for retirement.

PRETEND THAT THE STOCK MARKET DOES NOT EXIST

I think a strong case can be made to ignore the stock market altogether when it comes to saving for retirement. The risk of stock market disaster is simply too great. This is especially true if you start saving late, because there is less time to recover from a stock market crash. So how do you ignore the stock market? Pretend it doesn't even exist.

That's correct—every dollar you invest from now on goes into 100% no-risk government-guaranteed fixed-income GICs.

THE RRSP FALLACY

During the Spending Years when we are in debt, they ask us to make RRSP contributions, don't they? In fact, they want us to start as early as possible. You know, to realize the benefits of "compounding."

The truth is that these clever word plays make the product-pushers rich . . . and you poor.

How so? Well, since we are in debt, the only way we can make those RRSP contributions is by borrowing to do it. In other words, if you take $1,000 from your chequing account to make an RRSP contribution, you are borrowing to do it at the highest interest rate you have because that $1,000 could have otherwise gone to reduce your highest interest debt. All that debt you have is compounding, too—against you. It is compounding to the benefit of the financial institution that extended the loan to you.

Here's a simple example. Tom has $10,000 of credit card debt at an interest rate of 20% a year. He has a marginal tax rate of 40% (for each additional dollar he earns he pays $0.40 in tax and for each dollar he contributes to an RRSP he gets a $0.40 refund). I'll assume the RRSP contribution is made on January 2 and grows at 5% a year and that the earnings are added to the RRSP account on December 31. I'll also assume any credit card interest is paid before the last day of the year.

Case 1: RRSP Contribution (Year 1)

	January 1, Year 1	Cash In (Out) During Year	December 31, Year 1
RRSP Balance	$0		$10,500
RRSP Contribution		($10,000)	
RRSP Tax Refund		$4,000	
Credit Card Balance	($10,000)		($10,000)
Pay Down Credit Card		$0	
Credit Card Interest Expense		($2,000)	
Bank Balance	$14,000	($8,000)	$6,000
Net Worth	$4,000		$6,500

Case 2: Pay Down Credit Card (Year 1)

	January 1, Year 1	Cash In (Out) During Year	December 31, Year 1
RRSP Balance	$0	$0	$0
RRSP Contribution		$0	
RRSP Tax Refund		$0	
Credit Card Balance	($10,000)		$0
Pay Down Credit Card		($10,000)	
Credit Card Interest Expense		$0	
Bank Balance	$14,000	($10,000)	$4,000
Net Worth	$4,000		$4.000

At first glance it appears the RRSP is the way to go. Your after-tax cash outflow during the year is only $8,000 in case 1 versus $10,000 in case 2. Your net worth also is higher—$6,500 versus $4,000 under case 2. Stop here at your peril, as there is much more to the story than that.

What about year 2? Here are the charts:

Case 1: RRSP Contribution (Year 2)

	January 1, Year 2	Cash In (Out) During Year	December 31, Year 2
RRSP Balance	$10,500		$11,025
RRSP Contribution		$0	
RRSP Tax Refund		$0	
Credit Card Balance	($10,000)		($10,000)
Pay Down Credit Card		$0	
Credit Card Interest Expense		($2,000)	
Bank Balance	$6,000	($2,000)	$4,000
Net Worth	$6,500		$5,025

Case 2: Pay Down Credit Card (Year 2)

	January 1, Year 2	Cash In (Out) During Year	December 31, Year 2
RRSP Balance	$0	$0	$0
RRSP Contribution		$0	
RRSP Tax Refund		$0	
Credit Card Balance	$0		$0
Net Cash Inflow (Outflow)		$0	$0
Bank Balance	$4,000		$4,000
Net Worth	$4,000		$4,000

Can you see the problem with the RRSP strategy? Each and every year after year 1, in this case, $2,000 is continuing to flow out to the credit card company while your RRSP grows at only 5%. Look at the net worth of the RRSP strategy after year 1 and compare it to year 2. It has declined by $1,475 from $6,500 to $5,025. That's because $2,000 in interest has gone to the credit card company while the RRSP has grown by only $525. Meanwhile the pay down credit card net worth has remained at $4,000.

Say Tom carries his credit card debt from year to year. After five more years he will have paid $10,000 in interest. That's a huge amount of cash to be pouring down the drain.

That's the RRSP fallacy. Each and every year you are in debt, real cash is being drained from your bank account. Even if it's not credit card debt at 20%, it's probably at something higher than the actual return you are getting on your RRSP. But of course, they don't tell you what you're making on your RRSP do they? Could it be 5%, 8%, 10%? Well, in 2008, many people's investments posted significant negative figures—their RRSP might be worth less than the dollars they put in.

The conclusion is simple: if you've got credit card debt, forget about making an RRSP contribution.

Compound This

The next time your mutual fund salesperson uses the "benefits of compounding" argument to try to convince you to hand over more hard-earned cash for him to play with, remind him that you still have debt and therefore compounding is eating away at you.

Yes, I agree you should realize the benefits of compounding, but do it simply with no risk. That is, by paying off all debt, including your house mortgage, before investing another dime in your RRSP.

THE TAX TURBO-CHARGED RRSP

One of the main advantages of a delayed RRSP strategy is taxes. This is because since you are debt free, you'll have a significant amount of cash to make a large RRSP contribution and that contribution will lead to a large tax refund because you'll probably be in your peak earnings years at the highest tax bracket you'll ever be in. Each year's refund will be immediately reinvested in your RRSP, leading to significantly increased contributions.

Instead of trying to benefit from compounding that requires you to save for decades, use the benefit of taxes to get where you'd like to be without risk. Let's dig a little deeper, shall we?

A Word About Your RRSP Limit

First and foremost, it is important to note that all the RRSP room you built up during the early years where you were making earned income for RRSP purposes but not making RRSP contributions carries forward. In other words, if you were eligible to contribute $15,000 each year for ten years, and you didn't, after the ten-year period you would have accumulated $150,000 of RRSP room.

The amount you have accumulated is shown on your annual Notice of Assessment that the federal government mails you after reviewing your income tax return each year. It's usually shown at the bottom of one of the pages in a box titled "RRSP Deduction Limit Statement" and it looks like this:

Date	Name		Social insurance no.	Tax year	Tax centre
May 12, 2009	PAT SMITH		111 222 333	2008	Sudbury ON P3A 5C1

2009 RRSP Deduction Limit Statement

The back of this notice contains important information. Amounts marked with an asterisk (*) cannot be less than zero.

RRSP deduction limit for 2008		$5,000
Minus: Allowable RRSP contributions deducted in 2008		$5,000
Unused RRSP deduction limit at the end of 2008		$0
Plus: 18% of 2008 earned income of $44,444 = (max. $21,000). $8,000		
Minus: 2008 pension adjustment . . . . $0 . .		$8,000 *
		$8,000
Minus: 2009 net past service pension adjustment		$0
Plus: 2009 pension adjustment reversal		$0
Your **RRSP deduction limit for 2009**		$8,000 *(A)

You have $0 **(B)** of unused RRSP contributions available for 2009. If this amount is more than amount **(A)** above, you may have to pay a tax on excess contributions

See the bottom figure (A)? That's the key to the Tax Turbo-Charged RRSP. Don't worry that it is building up year after year; it's RRSP room that you'll use later.

DO YOU TRUST THE STOCK MARKET?

But hold on a minute. We've just been through 2008, and it showed the major weakness of the traditional RRSP strategy of starting early and trusting the stock market: in a matter of months your whole plan could be decimated.

The end of 2008 has also had a large impact on the often-quoted 6% to 8% average rate of return that the Canadian stock market has generated over the long term. Let's look at that.

In December 1983, the S&P/TSX Composite Index was at 2,537. In June 2008, it peaked at 15,073. During that twenty-five-year time span the average annual rate of return was 7.4%. On December 31, 2008, the index had declined to 8,987. The twenty-five-year average annual rate of return had declined to only 5.2%.

I have used a 5% average rate of return on many of the examples in this book. Based on what has just happened, that could be a pipe dream going forward. Besides the possibility of lower returns in the future, there are two factors that may draw average equity-based portfolios down to rates available with GICs.

The two reasons are fees and the need to diversify risk. Let me explain.

Those Ugly Fees

The main reason I have assumed a 5% rate of return throughout this book is because I am factoring in fees. In other words, if the stock market (equities) makes 7% a year during your investing horizon, and you use a typical Canadian equity mutual fund to try and get that return, you'll pay about 2% of that return in fees to the mutual fund company through the management expenses of that company. That leaves you with only a 5% return.

The new reality is that stock market returns may only be around 5%. Take off fees and you'll only get 3%.

Don't Put All Your Eggs in One Basket

But having 100% in equities is an extremely risky strategy. As we have just seen you could lose almost 40% of your nest egg in a matter of months. That's why many mutual fund sales people recommend that you diversify your asset mix. That means you should include a safe fixed-income component.

Say you decide to leave 65% of your portfolio in equity mutual funds at 5% return a year and 35% of your portfolio in safe GICs at 3% return a year. Your weighted average rate of return is as follows:

$$= (5\% \times 65\%) + (3\% \times 35\%)$$
$$= 4.3\%$$

Maybe even 5% is too high to use as an average expected rate of return for a well-balanced portfolio.

CONCLUSION

No one is sure whether the next twenty, thirty or fifty years will return the same results as the market has over the last twenty, thirty or fifty— a period of significant real economic growth after World War II.

What happens if the future is not so rosy?

Unfortunately the answer is not pretty. If you believe you can earn 5% a year on average after fees in your RRSP over the time you have left to retirement, and you actually do make 5%, your plan may work.

The problem is, will you actually realize that rate? And what if you, like all the other stock market believers, have suffered the crash of 2008? What used to look like an easily achievable goal of 5% a year now seems in doubt. Many are left wondering if they'll ever even get back to the amount they originally invested—they'd be a happy with a 0% rate of return!

Even if the future brings us back to the level of prosperity that our parents enjoyed, you may be better off forgetting the whole stock market thing and leaving it to the large financial institutions that know how it works like the back of their hand.

For me, I'd rather not spend the rest of my life worrying about what the stock market might do. I'd rather sleep at night knowing that it makes absolutely no difference to me or my family.

YOU MAY NOT NEED AN INVESTMENT ADVISOR

Don't get me wrong here—I strongly recommend that you use an investment advisor.

There are significant advantages to having a good one working for you, including

- **It takes time.** How many spare hours do you have each day to devote to your personal finances? Yeah, that's what I thought. We are all busy and having someone else doing the work for us simply makes sense if we are unlikely to spend the time ourselves.
- **Expertise is needed.** The more investment products and financial schemes you get involved in, the more you'll need to know about how they work. Good investment advisors will spend much of their daily working life researching the many products and options available, and using their experience and skills to make decisions. Will you be able to do the same?
- **Emotion is your enemy.** If you do all your own investing you'll probably find that, like many humans, greed and fear often get in the way of good investing habits. For example, if you were brilliant enough to pick a stock that doubled in price in one year, when do you pull the trigger and sell it? Many people suffer

large financial losses by waiting too long to sell a winner or sell-ing a loser before it rebounds.

There are many good, qualified investment advisors out there and you should spend the time and effort to try and find one.

The problem is finding one. Many people use their friends, rela-tives or even neighbours. That can be a recipe for disaster.

MY STORY

I'd like to tell you my story not because I am a particularly great inves-tor or so that you will follow what I did. I'd like to tell you because I think it has some important lessons and has actual numbers that re-ally happened.

I started making RRSP contributions in February 1991 when I was thirty-two years old. Just like many of you I started with the big bank that my parents had always used and invested in the bank's balanced equity mutual funds. I did this again in 1992.

In 1993, I listened to the siren call of these new mutual fund com-panies that were starting to emerge. Boy, they had great advertising! I bought into my first one that year.

In 1994, I was introduced to a new tax savings opportunity—Labour-Sponsored Investment Funds (LSIFs). At the time you could invest up to $5,000 a year and get a 20% federal and a 20% Ontario tax credit, for a $2,000 refund. That sounded good to me. I bought into one.

The lure of the tax refund was so strong that I continued to buy LSIFs in 1995 and 1996.

It was also at this time that I ran into the brother of a friend of mine who happened to work at a big brokerage firm. Since I was busy at work and investments seemed to be getting more and more compli-cated, I decided to transfer my self-directed holdings at several different banks and mutual fund companies to him.

From 1997 until 2002, I religiously drank the Kool-Aid of tradi-tional retirement advice and made RRSP contributions through thick and thin.

Here is a summary of the contributions I made, including the LSIF tax refunds I received.

Date Contributed	Amount Contributed	LSIF Refund	Net Amount Contributed	Invested With
2/28/1991	$4,000.00	$0.00	$4,000.00	Bank Balanced Equity Fund
2/28/1992	$4,000.00	$0.00	$4,000.00	Bank Balanced Equity Fund
2/28/1993	$6,000.00	$0.00	$6,000.00	Mutual Fund Co. #1
2/28/1994	$5,177.50	$2,000.00	$3,177.50	Mutual Fund Co. #2
2/28/1995	$5,000.00	$2,000.00	$3,000.00	LSIF
2/28/1996	$5,000.00	$1,050.00	$3,950.00	LSIF
2/28/1997	$5,000.00	$1,050.00	$3,950.00	Broker ($3,500 LSIF #1)
2/28/1998	$5,000.00	$1,500.00	$3,500.00	Broker ($3,500 LSIF #2)
7/31/1998	$7,500.00		$7,500.00	Broker
2/28/1999	$8,000.00	$1,500.00	$6,500.00	Broker ($5,000 LSIF #3)
2/28/2000	$10,000.00	$1,500.00	$8,500.00	Broker ($5,000 LSIF #4)
2/28/2001	$12,000.00	$0.00	$12,000.00	Broker ($5,000 LSIF #5)
3/1/2002	$5,000.00	$0.00	$5,000.00	Broker
TOTALS	**$81,677.50**	**$10,600.00**	**$71,077.50**	

But there was a problem. In fact, there was more than one problem.

First of all, I never knew how well the investments were doing. I'd get statements showing "Book Value" and the month-end market value, but not the most important figure of all—my personal rate of return!

Whenever I asked for it, I got a convoluted answer about how complicated it was to compute. Sometimes I'd get a handwritten summary of estimated returns. In fact, whenever I had a conversation with this guy, it went on so long that I had to say I had a meeting just to get off the phone.

That's when, by poring over old tax returns, I made the summary you see above. I wanted to see how well I was doing since I started.

Now, to be fair, this guy inherited the balanced equity funds, and a couple of mutual funds and LSIFs that I had purchased from 1991 to 1996, but when I compared the actual contributions above to the market value of the entire portfolio on June 30, 2004, a value of $89,092.56, I was surprised to find out that even after factoring in the LSIF tax refunds my actual personal rate of return was only 3.28% a year.

To get the real rate of return you'd have to ignore the income tax refunds because they were funded by the government and had nothing to do with the return on the investments themselves. The real rate of return without the tax refunds was only 1.26%.

Here's where it gets interesting. During the same period of March 1991 to June 2004, the S&P/TSX Composite Index rose to 8,398 from 3,495—an average annual rate of return of 6.97%. I wasn't invested 100% in equities so I wouldn't expect to match that, but I was significantly invested in the stock market to the tune of more than 75%. Shouldn't I have expected a return far above 1%?

What I Did Next

I knew I was not getting the results I desired or the service I needed, but there was a problem. I didn't want to take full responsibility for my own investing, especially since I was stuck in a lot of stuff that was not transparent and including all those LSIFs.

So I stayed with the original advisor even though I decided to stop making RRSP contributions.

A few years later I was lucky enough to come across an advisor who was a Chartered Accountant (CA) like me and even worked at the same CA firm that I did. He was the author of several books on investing and I attended a course he taught at the Institute of Chartered Accountants of Ontario (ICAO). We got to know each other and he offered to do a free portfolio review of my accounts.

The result was a large spreadsheet listing each investment, the category it was in (fixed income, Canadian equity, foreign equity, LSIF, etc.), the DSC fee to get out of each investment, the date when each would be free from a DSC, and the date when each LSIF would be free from having to pay back the income tax refund.

The results clearly showed I was more than 80% high risk and that I could get out of a significant number of investments DSC free. Together we began the slow process of getting out of the "dog" mutual funds and getting to the safety of GICs, government bonds and some low-fee bond funds.

This took place over the years, to the point where the entire portfolio structure was reversed so that 80% was fixed income and only 20% was exposed to the stock market. As a result, the fall of 2008 was not as devastating to me as to others.

WHAT TO LOOK FOR
IN AN INVESTMENT ADVISOR

When selecting an investment advisor, you should obviously look for someone who is well educated and has qualifications directly related to personal finances. I would also suggest that you look for someone with experience in up and down markets. Trusting your family's nest egg to a hotshot twenty-five-year-old is courting disaster.

Beyond that, I would pay particular attention to what the potential advisor has to say in your first few face-to-face meetings. Does he or she:

- Listen to your questions and provide simple answers?
- Ask about all the other things in your life, like your housing situation, debt levels and plans for retirement, or does he just zero in on your investments?
- Seem overly friendly and want to chat about your kids, hobbies and other interests? Many advisors are great at emotional selling, but you don't want to *be sold*—you want to buy some good independent expertise.

Then ask what he or she thinks of Canada's retirement system— the CPP and OAS pensions. Those who say it's at risk of not surviving may be trying to scare you into investing more with them.

DO YOU HAVE A LOUSY ADVISOR?

You probably already know if you've got a lousy advisor. The market value of your portfolio seems to go up sometimes but most often it goes down. He doesn't return your phone calls to explain why. Your investment statements show no evidence of how well your investments are doing, but they do contain confusing and contradictory descriptions for products, such as "monthly income" for high-risk equity stuff. You've therefore got no idea of how much you are exposed to high-risk products—is it 80% when it should be less than 20%?

NO ADVISOR IS BETTER THAN A BAD ONE

The truth is that if you stick to the concepts laid out in this book— avoid disasters, buy a home, pay for an expert to handle your taxes, only invest in what you can understand, and pay off all debt before you retire—you don't need to find that elusive investment advisor that you can trust with your family's future.

Because the plan is so simple, you can do it yourself. It won't keep you up at night.

HENRY'S STORY

I have my own ideas about the usefulness of an investment advisor, but I wanted to get the first-hand experiences of an expert. I wanted to find someone who had been trained in the world of finance and worked in the financial sector for at least thirty years, someone who had experience with his own personal finances and used various investment brokers both at work and personally. This person would also have to believe in the stock market.

I found such a person in a family friend that I'll call Henry. Here is Henry's story in his own words:

Dear David:

You asked me to provide my views on personal financial invest-ing. My views were developed from thirty years in the finance function in the business world after getting my MBA and by the experiences I have had myself with personal investments.

Initially I worked in a manufacturing company with a global "empire" and a Canadian operation (Company #1) that pretended to be independent. Nevertheless, the financial training program was excellent and I became heavily involved in the Treasury function. Company #2 was considered to be at the forefront of managing pension investments.

The global Company #1 had done a study that measured the performance of a dozen of the best pension managers in the world. Over a period of ten years these managers had the unfettered discretion to move money between fixed-income and equity markets. Not remembering exactly the actual numbers, if in the measurement period the real rate of return on fixed investments was 3% and the real rate of return on equity investments was 5%, one would expect the portfolio managers would achieve a return somewhere between 3% and 5%. As it turned out, the best efforts of the collective wisdom of a dozen of the best pension managers who could be retained by a global household-name empire turned in actual returns notably under 3%. Throw a dart at a board with random scattered numbers from one to one hundred. Use the dart landing point to establish the equity/fixed-income mix at time zero. If you want, at the last minute, reverse the number to fixed-income/equity mix. Whichever choice you make, hold that mix and by the end of the period you will beat the average of the managers. As a consequence, by the time I became involved, Company #1 had turned the first corner and managed the fixed-income/equity mix itself, leaving the content of the equity portfolio to the outside experts. This experience encouraged me to create Principle #1 in my thinking.

Principle #1: No one can time the markets

In the seventies and early eighties Company #1 focused heavily on relative performance of external managers in the equity markets. Every quarter we prepared charts and packages with comparisons among our seven or eight managers, showing actual absolute *returns and actual returns versus the stock exchanges and against other managers for annual, four-year and four-year rolling returns, and returns for each manager from the beginning of time.*

The first portion of most meetings was dedicated to complaints about data inaccuracies. Then the managers would explain the troughs and spikes in their charts. The spikes were usually the result of their unique clever actions (e.g., methanol prices rise globally and methanol stocks go up dramatically). Any pension manager holding such stock gets credit. Meanwhile, managers without such stocks are grilled by the company representatives. Our goal was to get an answer to the question: "How could you be so out of touch as to not buy methanol stocks?" We interviewed potential new managers steadily, mostly by their own initiative. They all had certain skills—rarely acquired in any actual industry job, but at hard work in business schools, investment companies and banks where they developed personal skills of magnitude.

After several years of this process I learned that the managers really had very little capability of picking stocks successfully to beat other managers or stock market indices. They did their best and kept trying "new approaches": technical, contrary, value, large cap, small cap and many others. They tried showing unique measuring periods—all performance measurements are so sensitive to starting and ending periods—it was often possible to find some good news in any mess. They brought in their research people from the back room. Some of them had good runs but the inevitability was always there and one major offside decision could get them fired. Mostly they weathered the stormy periods and basked in invisibility in the good periods.

In this period I developed Principle #2 in my thinking.

Principle #2: Today's hero is tomorrow's loser

In the early eighties I moved to Company #2, where I had less involvement with pensions but what I did see was more of the same in terms of investment performance. The Company set the

equity/fixed income mix and used external managers to man-
age the equity funds. Principles #1 and #2 were re-validated.
By the end of my stay at Company #2 equity index funds had
made their entry into the portfolio.

Although it has nothing to do with individual personal invest-
ing, one of my responsibilities at Company #2 was to obtain
approval for the actuarial rate that would determine the pension
expense applied against profits. This was like the blind leading
the blind. The Corporate sponsors were motivated to maximize
profits; therefore, a higher rate was more desirable. Meanwhile,
the experts, who could not time anything and were on their way
to being heroes or bums, added their input, generally preferring
a low rate—an easier target to beat in the future. External audi-
tors grumbled but generally agreed with management.

In the mid-nineties I became CFO of a Canadian-based multi-
national public company—Company #3. By this time I had
seen enough and pushed aggressively to move to index funds
for the equity portion of the fund. The Company did not man-
age any funds directly and also used external managers to
administer the index funds at substantially lower fees. Index
funds can duplicate the "averages" quite successfully and accu-
rately. Because there is no opportunity to add value and charge
enormous fees, pension investment managers were obviously
reluctant to acknowledge the value of index funds.

Principle #3: People on commission cannot be trusted

This principle applies in the investment world as well. You have
to understand the priorities of your advisor. Clearly, the first
priority is himself and his career and what that means for his
family. More than likely, his second priority is his employer,
who is very important to our advisor's future. And clearly, the
third priority is the client.

So, now we have in total an advisor who has no way to time
markets or pick stocks effectively. Furthermore, his priorities are

not totally aligned with yours. He is bright, well educated, and intelligent and you are going to put your financial security in his hands. The best you can hope for is a win/win/win outcome because if any one person doesn't win, the highest probability is that you are the loser—win/win/lose.

Of course, they want your repeat business, but the primary responsibility of your investment advisor is to get you to buy or sell something, anything. You want my ideas? Your ideas? What the firm recommends? Guess what the firm recommends? Paper it issues for its corporate clients is top priority. At the Monday morning Sales meeting the troops are brought in and told this week they have to peddle W shares of X Corporation or $Y million of Z Corporation notes. Step right up, troops. The more you take on the more you impress your boss and your cohorts in the room. You know you will be able to stuff it into accounts of unwary or overly trusting clients.

Henry's Personal Investments

With the above background, here is what happened with one of our portfolios. It is non-registered, and was initially established as an investment portfolio and latterly as a vehicle to generate income. The portfolio was started with $500,000 in late 1994 and early 1995 and was given to a brokerage related to one of the "big five" banks. The broker had to clear investments with me and I planned to keep equities under 50%. After five years the account had reached $750,000. Investments in equities averaged roughly 30% of the total portfolio. A summary of the transactions:

1. *The broker bought thirteen individual stocks with an average investment of $17,000. The thirteen stocks were held for a weighted average of 550 days. In the five-year period, ten had been sold, four at a loss and six at a gain.*
2. *Of the three stocks still held at the end of the five-year period, two were down 21% and 88% and one was up 33%.*

3. The average net capital gain was 13% on the thirteen stocks picked by the broker (excluding any dividends received).
4. Roughly four thousand TSE equity index shares were purchased in the five years. None were sold, and by the end of the five-year measuring period the index had been owned for a weighted average of 750 days. Over the five-year period the capital gain on the index shares was 49% (excluding any dividends received).
5. Interest income averaged over 5% per year.

If all of the stock investments by the broker had been made in equity index funds the portfolio would have been worth $75,000 more at the end of the five-year period. For this performance and particularly for buying Loewen (down 73%) and Laidlaw (down 88%), I moved the funds to another brokerage related to another of the "big five" banks. New cash of $190,000 and a portfolio with a market value of $750,000 from Broker 1 were handed to Broker 2 early in 2000.

Through December 31, 2007, here's what the broker accomplished:

1. Bought thirteen different income trust units and all were sold by December 31, 1997. The average investment was $26,000 and the overall net capital gain was 6% over the period. This is only the gain/loss on share purchases and sales and does not include dividends received or additional tax benefits.
2. Bought two equity mutual funds for $70,000 in 2001, which were down in capital value by 16% and were still in the portfolio at December 31, 2007.
3. Bought and sold through the period fifteen individual stocks with an average investment of $20,000 each. Twelve were sold generating capital gains and three were sold generating capital losses. The average capital net gain was 6%.
4. Inherited four thousand equity index shares from Broker 1 and within eighteen months sold most of them, generating a net loss of roughly $10,000.

5. *Bought at my request one individual stock we thought would have value. After holding it for three plus years it was sold for nickels. It is now trading for pennies.*

6. *Put into our portfolio an investment double the size of the normal investments we would make. The investment structure was far more complex than anything we had ever bought and should never have made it into our portfolio, but I did approve it in a brief telephone conversation. Immediately after issue it started to fade. Less than a year later it was sold for a loss of $15,000. I believe I was victimized by the Monday morning Sales meeting and the need for the broker to sell $Y million of the notes the broker's firm was issuing for Corporation Z.*

In the latter half of the measurement period monthly withdrawals were made, which undoubtedly caused some disruption. In total, during the period following when Broker #2 started, net cash withdrawals totalled $450,000.

Over the whole period, capital gains and capital losses netted to a trivial number. Dividend, interest and investment income was almost $400,000 and the portfolio ended at about $900,000. If none of the individual stocks, income trusts and personal stock picks had been made and the investments in the original four thousand index shares had been held to December 31, 2007, the original investment of $150,000 would have grown to $325,000—a gain of $175,000. In this period, the two Brokers together made investments of $1.25 million in individual stocks and realized a capital gain of $50,000.

Lessons I draw from this review:

1. *Principles #2 and #3 are validated by my personal experience.*

2. *I have to be more forceful in directing the portfolio in the direction I want, e.g., buying index shares. In spite of telling both brokers in advance that I was strongly in favour of*

*equity funds, I believe neither of them ever recommended
an investment in equity index funds.*

3. *I have to be more vigilant—do not allow the Monday
   morning Sales meeting to affect me again.*

Soon I will retire and devote more time to my investments.

CONCLUSION

Well, that's Henry's story. A professional investor's experience during
the past few decades of the ups and downs of the stock market. He
concludes that active management of a portfolio usually doesn't even
match the index—the return you would have received without any
advice at all.

If you still believe the stock market is the way to secure your retirement, do you really think you can do better than Henry by using your
current investment advisor in the lean years to come?

PART TWO
THE DETAILS

Well there you have it—The Antidote—a six-point plan to guide you through the financial storm we are in. Remember, pick and choose what feels right for you. You don't have to follow all six steps in order. You don't even have to follow all six points. Follow even one and you'll probably improve your personal financial situation significantly.

Now let's go one step further—the details. In this section we'll explore the ins and outs of the CPP. We'll discover a concrete answer to the question about what age you should choose to start to receive it at. We'll also discover a tip that can save you thousands of dollars each and every year.

We'll also learn about the Money Maximizer spreadsheet and how to use this tool to maximize the money you and your family get to keep. I'll show you how you can get a free copy of it as a reader of this book.

We'll also address how to recover from the stock market crash of 2008 and the best ways to maximize your retirement income in this new economic reality we all face.

Lastly we'll look at alternatives to RRSPs. Can anything beat them? You'll know soon.

7

THE CANADA PENSION PLAN QUESTION

WHAT IS THE CANADA PENSION PLAN?

The Canada Pension Plan (CPP) is a mandatory government-sponsored pension plan that came into effect on January 1, 1966 and was fully implemented on January 1, 1976. The only province that does not use the CPP is Quebec. They opted to create their own plan, the Quebec Pension Plan (QPP), which is similar to the CPP but supported by the provincial government.

The CPP is funded by Canadians that are employees, employers or self-employed. Contributions are required as soon as you reach the age of eighteen and are no longer required after you either reach the age of seventy, become disabled or start receiving a CPP retirement pension.

Under the CPP, monthly pensions are paid to retirees, surviving spouses or common-law partners of deceased contributors, orphans, the disabled and children of the disabled. The term "common-law partners" came into force on July 30, 2000 and replaced the former term "spouse." This change broadened the entitlement to survivor's benefits to partners in same-sex relationships. A common-law partner is defined for CPP purposes as a person who is cohabiting with the contributor in a conjugal relationship at the relevant time, having so cohabited with the contributor for a continuous period of at least one year.

Lump-sum death benefits are also paid to the estate of deceased contributors. The amount is dependent on the contributions the deceased made to the CPP during his or her lifetime. The maximum lump-sum death benefit is currently $2,500.

It is important to note that the monthly benefits paid under the plan are adjusted annually, based on increases in the Consumer Price Index (CPI), the most common measure of inflation in Canada. In short, the CPP is an inflation-adjusted defined benefit pension plan that is paid until you die.

HOW THEY CALCULATE CPP PREMIUMS

Regular CPP premiums for employees are calculated at a rate of 4.95% of earnings above an exemption of $3,500 to a maximum of $44,900 in 2008. In other words, if you make under $3,500 you pay no CPP premiums and the maximum you pay is based on earnings up to $44,900—if you earn more than that you only pay premiums on $44,900.

Here are the key figures for 2008:

Yearly Maximum Pensionable Earnings (YMPE)	$44,900.00
Yearly Basic Exemption	$3,500.00
Yearly Maximum Contributory Earnings	$41,400.00 ($44,900 less $3,500)
Yearly Maximum Contributions	$2,049.30 ($41,400.00 × 4.95%)

HOW THEY CALCULATE THE CPP PENSION

You may be wondering how they calculate the maximum monthly CPP retirement pension. It's pretty straightforward. It's 25% of the last five years' average maximum pensionable earnings (AMPE).

Here's how they got the maximum monthly CPP retirement pension for 2008.

Last five years' YMPE:

2004	$40,500
2005	$41,100
2006	$42,100
2007	$43,700

2008 $44,900

Average of 2004 to 2008 YMPE (AMPE)	$42,460
25% of the AMPE	$10,615
Monthly ($10,615/12)	$884.58

HOW THE CPP ADJUSTS FOR INFLATION: THE YMPE

The YMPE is increased each year by the ratio of the average industrial aggregate (average weekly earnings), as determined by Statistics Canada, during the twelve-month period ending June 30 of the preceding year, to the average industrial aggregate during the corresponding period one year earlier.

The YMPE increased by 2.75% from 2007 to 2008 ($44,900 − $43,700 = $1,200, divided by $43,700 = 2.75%) because the average weekly earnings increased from $738.13 (July 2005 to June 2006) to $758.45 (July 2006 to June 2007) ($758.45 − $738.13 = $20.32, divided by $738.13 = 2.75%).

This calculation is used to obtain the percentage increase, which is applied to the 2007 YMPE to obtain the 2008 unrounded YMPE ($43,700 × 1.0275 = $44,901.75). To obtain the official YMPE, the unrounded YMPE is truncated and rounded down to the nearest $100 ($44,900).

CPP Pension

It is only after you begin to receive the CPP pension that the CPP uses the CPI to adjust your CPP pension amount. These increases are included so that contributions and benefits keep up with the cost of living.

Statistics Canada developed the CPI to measure changes in the cost of living. The main CPI is called the Total CPI. It tracks the prices of a basket of approximately six hundred items, including typical household expenditures such as food, clothing, shelter, transportation and recreation, on a monthly basis.

They used to use 1992 as the base year for calculations but now they use 2002. That is to say, the CPI index was made equal to 100 in June of 2002. This means that the defined basket of goods cost $100 in June 2002. The Total CPI index was 115.5 in August 2008, meaning that same basket of goods would have cost $115.50 at that time.

The CPP pension is adjusted once a year using a twelve-month "moving average method," which helps to smooth out fluctuations that may occur in a single month. The rate used to increase the CPP pension is the average monthly Total CPI index for the prior year's twelve-month period ending in October. They use October because they need to publish the rates for the next year in the fall of the previous year.

Here's how they got the rate to increase existing CPP pensions for 2008:

- average Total CPI Index of all months November 2006 to October 2007 = 111.0
- average Total CPI Index of all months November 2005 to October 2006 = 108.8

The percentage increase is 2.0% (111.0 − 108.8 = 2.2, divided into 108.8 = 2.0%).

Here's the good news: if the cost of living decreases over the twelve-month periods, the calculation of the rate increase would produce a negative amount but the CPP pension does not decrease in this case. It stays at the prior year's level.

Here's the bad news: Your CPP contribution rates increase every year by inflation, but since the retirement pension is calculated on the last five years' YMPE, it may lag current inflation.

YOU MUST APPLY TO START RECEIVING IT

In order to start receiving the CPP pension, you must make an application on a specified form. Although it is not a requirement, the government suggests you apply for your CPP pension six months before you want your pension to begin. Payment of the benefit also must be approved by the government.

Applying to receive the CPP is an important step that some seniors are not aware of. There are many seniors that are out of pocket because they simply have not filled in the form. If you know any seniors, especially those newer to the country that may not speak either language very well, do them a favour and make sure they are receiving the CPP if they are eligible. It could make a significant difference to some of them.

Application kits are available from the Human Resources and Social Development Canada (HRSDC) website at http://www.hrsdc.gc.ca, or you can call 1-800-277-9914 (English) or 1-800-277-9915 (French) to have a kit mailed to you. The government has also made the application Web-based. You can find it by googling "Canada Pension Plan Retirement Application." This allows you to complete the process quickly and efficiently.

You can also do this online using the "My Service Canada Account."

MY SERVICE CANADA ACCOUNT

The federal government makes certain information and forms available over the Internet using a service called "My Service Canada Account." It's available from the Service Canada website (http://www.servicecanada .gc.ca). It provides a one-stop service by offering Service Canada online services through a single access point. This initiative is part of a plan to harmonize services and business processes between Service Canada and other government departments.

My Service Canada Account brings together CPP, Old Age Security (OAS) and Employment Insurance (EI) online services into a single portal. You can

- apply for the CPP Retirement pension
- view your CPP Statement of Contributions online
- view tax information slips for CPP, OAS and EI
- apply for a personal access code for CPP and OAS
- access EI services
- manage Records of Employment
- change your personal information (update your mailing address, telephone number, direct deposit information, etc.)

My Service Canada Account also includes links to other online services that are available outside the portal, such as the online CPP Retirement Application and the Canadian Retirement Income Calculator.

My Service Canada Account epass

A My Service Canada Account epass will enable you to enter a user ID and password to login to your My Service Canada Account. Here's how to obtain your user ID and password for future visits.

From the My Service Canada Account home page just mentioned, you will need to select "Access My Service Canada Account," select the same phrase again and then choose "Register for My Service Canada Account" to begin the registration process. You will then need to complete the following four steps in order to obtain an epass user ID and password. This is a one-time-only process.

1. Read the explanation of the registration process, which consists of creating a user ID, a password and recovery questions, answers and hints.
2. Create a user ID and recovery questions (the user ID needs to be no more than sixteen characters, can include no more than seven digits and can't include special characters like @, %, #).
3. Create a password (it must be eight to sixteen characters, and have at least one upper case and lower case letter and a digit).
4. Accept the Terms and Conditions of Use by entering the new password and selecting the option "Sign."

Once you have completed the four steps listed above you will be presented with an epass welcome page with a "Continue" button.

After choosing "Continue," you will be brought to the Service Canada registration and validation process in order to validate your identity. Complete the following in order to register and validate your identity:

- your Social Insurance Number (SIN)
- your date of birth
- your EI access code or CPP/OAS personal access code
- your province or territory
- your epass password

After completing the steps to register for an epass and the steps to register and validate your identity with Service Canada, you will be presented with the My Service Canada Account home page. On subsequent visits, users will only need to provide their epass user ID and password to login to their My Service Canada Account.

HOW DO I KNOW HOW MUCH I'LL GET?

You can make a request to the government through Service Canada to get an estimate of your CPP retirement income. The form allows you to choose any two retirement ages from forty to seventy and to elect any two ages between sixty and seventy for your pension to begin. You can find the form at http://www.hrsdc.gc.ca/en/isp/cpp/soc/50-70/ yourcpp.shtml. Here's what the form looks like:

Service Canada

Protected when completed - A
Personal Information bank
HRSDC PPU 140 and 146

Estimate Request for Canada Pension Plan (CPP) Retirement Pension

It is very important that you:
- use a **pen** and **print** as clearly as possible

1A. Social Insurance Number	1B. Sex ○ Male ○ Female	1C. Date of Birth — Year Month Day

2. ○ Mr. ○ Mrs. ○ Ms. ○ Miss ▶ Usual First Name and Initial — Last Name

3. Mailing Address (No., Street, Apt., P.O. Box, R.R. and City) — Province or Territory / Country If other than Canada / Postal Code

Telephone Number(s) **4A.** Area code and telephone number at home — **4B.** Area code and telephone number at work (if applicable)

5. When you request an estimate of your Canada Pension Plan retirement pension, we automatically calculate the amount you will receive at age 65. However, you can receive a Canada Pension Plan retirement pension as early as age 60. If you expect to retire from the workforce before age 65, we can estimate the retirement pension you could receive when you retire. You can choose any two retirement ages between 40 and 70 for which you would like estimates.

NOTE : We reduce Retirement pensions paid to people **under** age 65 by 0.5% for each month the person is **under** 65 years of age. We increase Retirement pensions paid to people who begin receiving the pension when they are **over** age 65 by 0.5% for each month the person is **over** 65 years of age up to age 70. The maximum increase or decrease is 30%.

If retire at age [ ] (40 to 70) in Year Month [ ] **FIRST CHOICE:** , what will my **estimated** retirement pension be at age [ ] ? (60 to 70)

If retire at age [ ] (40 to 70) in Year Month [ ] **SECOND CHOICE:** , what will my **estimated** retirement pension be at age [ ] ? (60 to 70)

6. Did you or your spouse or common-law partner receive or were either of you eligible to receive Family Allowances or the Child Tax Benefit for any children born after December 31, 1958?

You ▶ ○ No ○ Yes ▶ Your spouse or common-law partner ▶ ○ No ○ Yes

If yes, enter the periods during which you or your spouse or common-law partner received the benefits. Also list the dates of birth of all children born after December 31st, 1958.

	FROM — Year Month Day	TO — Year Month Day	DATE OF BIRTH OF CHILD — Year Month Day
a)			
b)			

Note: Please use another sheet of paper if you have more than 2 children.

7. Have you at anytime received a Canada Pension Plan disability benefit? ○ No ○ Yes ▶ **If yes,** for what periods? FROM — Year Month Day — TO — Year Month Day

I understand that the above information is confidential and that you will use it to estimate the amount of my benefit. **I understand that this is not an application for a benefit.** Year Month Day

SIGNATURE X

Service Canada delivers Human Resources and Skills Development Canada programs and services for the Government of Canada.

SC-ISP1003(2009-04-006) E Disponible en fran•ais

Canada

MONEY-SAVING TIP: CPP PENSIONS

As we've discussed, the most important method of saving taxes in Canada is to optimize the split of income on the tax returns belonging to you, your spouse or common-law partner and your children. This also applies to the Canada Pension Plan.

Under the CPP, common-law partners or spouses in an ongoing relationship, who are both at least sixty years old and who receive CPP payments, can apply to share their CPP retirement pension payments by assigning a portion of the contributor's retirement income to his or her common-law partner or spouse.

Essentially, the government allows you to decide how much of one contributor's CPP pension can be shown on the other spouse's personal income tax return. The tax savings of this can be large, especially if one spouse has been the only breadwinner throughout the relationship.

You or your spouse or common-law partner can apply to receive an equal share of the retirement pensions you both earned during the years you were together. The amounts depend on how long you lived together and your contributions to the CPP during that time.

CPP Pension Sharing Example

Pension sharing adjusts the amount of the monthly CPP retirement pension each spouse or common-law partner receives from the CPP.

For example, if you lived together for twenty-five years during both your contributory periods:

- add together the pension earned by each of you during the twenty-five-year period
- divide it equally between you and your spouse or common-law partner
- each of you keeps the rest of your pension earned outside the time you lived together

Here's an example of how it works.

Kyle and Sue have been living together in a common-law relationship since 1979. They are both over sixty years old and both receive a CPP retirement pension.

Sue's monthly retirement pension is $400. Of that, $100 is based on income earned before moving in with Kyle; this amount will not be affected by a pension-sharing arrangement. The other $300 is based on income earned during their relationship.

Kyle was not working before this relationship. Kyle's monthly retirement pension of $550 is based entirely on income earned while living with Sue.

Their pension payments, added together, total $950. After subtracting the portion of Sue's pension that is based on income earned before moving in with Kyle ($100), their "shareable" pension amount is $850. With pension sharing, they would each receive half of $850, or $425. In addition to the $425, Sue would also receive the $100 that is based on earnings prior to this relationship with Kyle. Sue's total monthly CPP payment would be $525, while Kyle's would be $425.

Their T4A(P) – Statement of Canada Pension Plan Benefits slips will show the amount each received during the previous year and will be used when calculating their income tax.

Your pension-sharing arrangement stops:

- if both you and your spouse or common-law partner request an end to it
- the twelfth month after you separate
- the month you divorce or the marriage is annulled
- if one of you has never paid into the CPP (or QPP) and begins contributing
- the month one of you dies

Pension sharing only starts when your application is approved and the government does not allow you to backdate the sharing arrangement, so if it is of benefit to you, do not hesitate to apply. Either you or your spouse or common-law partner can apply.

The application form is available on the Web at http://www1 .servicecanada.gc.ca/en/isp/pub/factsheets/sharing.shtml. Note that the overall benefits paid do not increase or decrease with pension sharing.

WHEN SHOULD I ELECT TO RECEIVE CPP?

There is an important decision regarding the CPP that many Canadians aren't sure how to answer. It relates to when you should start receiving the CPP pension. The normal age is sixty-five but you can elect to receive it as early as age sixty. There is, however, a penalty of a reduction of 0.5% for each month that you elect to start receiving your pension before you turn sixty-five. That's 6% per year.

You can also elect to delay receiving the CPP pension until as late as age seventy. In this case you get a premium of 0.5% a month for each month you wait after you turn sixty-five.

So what age should you elect to start receiving your CPP pension?

Unfortunately, just like with any decision related to personal finance, there appears to be no easy answer. The main reason for this is that you need to know one important thing: when are you going to live until? Now that's a tough question to answer, isn't it? Yes it is, but it can make a big difference to the calculations.

For example, say you retire at age sixty and end up passing away at age sixty-seven. If you elected early, at age sixty, you would have received your CPP retirement pension (at a reduced rate of 70% of the full amount) for seven years. If you had waited until age sixty-five you would have only received the pension for two years. If you crunch these numbers you'd see that you'd be better off electing at age sixty since the greater number of years you collected the reduced pension outweighs the lesser number of years for the full one. Put simply, the reduction penalty of 30% of the amount at age sixty-five (five years early × 6%) is not overcome by waiting because you only get the higher rate for two years in this case.

On the other hand, if you actually live to the ripe old age of ninety-five, you'd think that it would be best to wait until age sixty-five to receive your CPP pension because you'd be receiving the full amount for twenty years.

But give me a few minutes and I'll show you that the answer isn't so complicated after all.

To help answer the question, I've created a spreadsheet that will allow you to figure it out for yourself. (It's available on my website at http://www.trahair.com.) Have a look at the following chart: Canada Pension Plan Total Income Comparison Chart. It shows the "Summary Chart" screen of the spreadsheet for someone who lives until any age between seventy-one and ninety-five.

Canada Pension Plan Total Income Comparison Chart

Death	Age 60	Age 61	Age 62	Age 63	Age 64	Age 65	**Maximum**	Elect Age
71	$136,259	$134,224	$130,313	$124,585	$117,095	$107,897	$136,259	Age 60
72	149,144	147,939	144,821	139,849	133,079	124,569	149,144	Age 60
73	162,286	161,928	159,618	155,417	149,384	141,574	162,286	Age 60
74	175,692	176,197	174,712	171,298	166,014	158,919	176,197	Age 61
75	189,365	190,751	190,107	187,495	182,977	176,611	190,751	Age 61
76	203,312	205,596	205,810	204,017	200,279	194,656	205,810	Age 62
77	217,537	220,738	221,827	220,869	217,928	213,063	221,827	Age 62
78	232,048	236,183	238,165	238,059	235,929	231,838	238,165	Age 62
79	246,848	251,937	254,829	255,592	254,290	250,988	255,592	Age 63
80	261,944	268,006	271,827	273,476	273,019	270,521	273,476	Age 63
81	277,343	284,397	289,165	291,717	292,122	290,445	292,122	Age 64
82	293,049	301,115	306,849	310,323	311,607	310,768	311,607	Age 64
83	309,069	318,167	324,887	329,301	331,482	331,497	331,497	Age 65
84	325,410	335,561	343,286	348,659	351,754	352,640	352,640	Age 65
85	342,078	353,303	362,053	368,404	372,432	374,206	374,206	Age 65
86	359,079	371,399	381,195	388,544	393,523	396,204	396,204	Age 65
87	376,420	389,857	400,720	409,087	415,036	418,641	418,641	Age 65
88	394,108	408,685	420,635	430,041	436,980	441,528	441,528	Age 65
89	412,149	427,889	440,949	451,414	459,362	464,872	464,872	Age 65
90	430,552	447,477	461,669	473,214	482,192	488,683	488,683	Age 65
91	449,322	467,456	482,804	495,450	505,478	512,970	512,970	Age 65
92	468,468	487,836	504,361	518,131	529,231	537,743	537,743	Age 65
93	487,997	508,623	526,349	541,265	553,458	563,011	563,011	Age 65
94	507,916	529,825	548,777	564,862	578,170	588,785	588,785	Age 65
95	$528,234	$551,452	$571,654	$588,932	$603,376	$615,074	$615,074	Age 65

Let's look at the first three lines of the chart. Let's say, for example, that you live to age seventy-one. If you had elected to receive the discounted CPP pension starting at age sixty, you would have received a total of $136,259 in CPP pension income. Waiting until sixty-five would have left you with only $107,897. You would have collected $28,362 more by starting at age sixty.

Let's say you live until age seventy-eight, the current life expectancy for males according to Statistics Canada. Electing at age sixty-two would have given you the maximum amount of pension: $238,165 versus $231,838 if you waited until age sixty-five.

As you can see, it's not until a lifespan of eighty-three years that waiting until age sixty-five yields the maximum pension.

Note that this spreadsheet illustration assumes inflation will be 2.00% per year (the CPP plan is indexed to inflation). When you use it you can input any inflation figure you wish.

THE TIME VALUE OF MONEY

But the spreadsheet we have just discussed ignores one vital thing: the time value of money. In a nutshell, this means that a dollar received today is worth more than in a year from now. Think about it, would you rather have a dollar today or a year from today? You'd rather have it today because you could spend it or perhaps invest it. At a return of 5% it would grow to $1.05 in a year. What would happen to the spreadsheet if we accounted for the time value of money and discounted the future CPP pension income cash flows in each case?

That would give us a real "apples to apples" comparison and, as well see, make your CPP decision a lot easier.

But what interest rate should we use? In business circles the interest rate (called the discount rate) is the business' "incremental cost of borrowing." That's the interest rate it would pay to invest in whatever it is that will provide the future cash inflows (e.g., a piece of equipment). In the case of an individual, that rate would be whatever the cost is of any debt they might have, or the investment return rate they think they might be able to achieve if they have no debt.

Let's say we are debt free and expect an annual rate of return on our investments of 5%. The table opposite shows the same results as the first table, but discounts the CPP pension received to current dollars at a rate of 5% per year.

Canada Pension Plan Total Income Comparison Chart NPV

Death	Age 60	Age 61	Age 62	Age 63	Age 64	Age 65	Maximum	Elect Age	Dollar Ben of Wait
71	$99,493	$95,604	$90,546	$84,450	$77,435	$69,614	$99,493	Age 60	$0
72	106,326	102,878	98,240	92,545	85,912	78,455	106,326	Age 60	0
73	112,964	109,943	105,714	100,408	94,147	87,044	112,964	Age 60	0
74	119,412	116,806	112,974	108,047	102,147	95,387	119,412	Age 60	0
75	125,676	123,474	120,027	115,467	109,917	103,492	125,676	Age 60	0
76	131,761	129,951	126,878	122,675	117,466	111,365	131,761	Age 60	0
77	137,672	136,243	133,533	129,678	124,800	119,014	137,672	Age 60	0
78	143,414	142,355	139,999	136,480	131,923	126,443	143,414	Age 60	0
79	148,992	148,292	146,279	143,088	138,843	133,661	148,992	Age 60	0
80	154,411	154,060	152,381	149,507	145,566	140,672	154,411	Age 60	0
81	159,675	159,663	158,307	155,743	152,096	147,483	159,675	Age 60	0
82	164,789	165,106	164,065	161,801	158,440	154,100	165,106	Age 61	317.60
83	169,756	170,394	169,658	167,685	164,603	160,527	170,394	Age 61	637.63
84	174,582	175,530	175,091	173,402	170,589	166,771	175,530	Age 61	948.52
85	179,269	180,520	180,369	178,955	176,405	172,836	180,520	Age 61	1,250.52
86	183,823	185,367	185,496	184,350	182,054	178,728	185,496	Age 62	1,673.56
87	188,246	190,075	190,477	189,590	187,542	184,452	190,477	Age 62	2,230.67
88	192,544	194,649	195,316	194,680	192,873	190,012	195,316	Age 62	2,771.87
89	196,718	199,093	200,016	199,626	198,052	195,413	200,016	Age 62	3,297.59
90	200,773	203,409	204,582	204,429	203,082	200,660	204,582	Age 62	3,808.30
91	204,713	207,602	209,017	209,096	207,969	205,757	209,096	Age 63	4,383.59
92	208,539	211,676	213,326	213,629	212,717	210,709	213,629	Age 63	5,090.13
93	212,257	215,632	217,511	218,033	217,329	215,519	218,033	Age 63	5,776.49
94	215,868	219,476	221,577	222,311	221,809	220,191	222,311	Age 63	6,443.24
95	$219,376	$223,210	$225,527	$226,467	$226,161	$224,730	$226,467	Age 63	7,090.94

Interesting. It seems that waiting to age sixty-five *never* yields the maximum CPP pension. Even if you live to age ninety-five, electing at age sixty-three would have left you better off by only $7,091 ($226,467 versus $219,376 versus electing at age 60).

This is where the decision gets easier. The answer to the question "When should I elect to receive CPP pension?" is "as soon as you retire."

Why wait? First of all, the numbers support it, but just as importantly, life happens.

My father-in-law, Jack, a great person and one of my closest friends, passed away at age sixty-eight. What about you? Are you willing to bet you'll make it to age eighty-two, ninety or ninety-five? Why bother waiting, especially when the benefit is so small? Live life while you can . . . and get the CPP to help.

STARTING THE CPP PENSION BEFORE SIXTY-FIVE

You can't simply elect to start receiving your CPP pension before age sixty-five; you need to do one of the following two things:

1. **Stop working.** For CPP purposes, this means that you are not working by the end of the month before the CPP retirement pension begins and during the month in which it begins. For example, if you request that your pension begins in June, you have to stop working by the end of May and you cannot work during the month of June.
2. **Have low earnings.** This means you need to be earning less than the current monthly maximum CPP retirement pension ($908.75 in 2009) in the month prior to the month your pension begins and in the month it begins. For example, if you had requested that your pension begin in December 2009, you would have needed to earn less than $908.75 in both November and December 2009.

MONEY-SAVING TIP: SELF-EMPLOYMENT INCOME

Once you start to receive your CPP pension, you can work as much as you want without affecting your pension payment and you are not required to contribute to CPP on any future earnings.

This presents a money saving opportunity.

Say you retire from your job at age sixty-two in early June of 2009, and for the reasons we have discussed you elect to start receiving your CPP pension in July of 2009 at the reduced rate. You don't want to completely leave the world of work and could use some extra cash. You decide to realize your dream of starting your own business and plan to start doing some consulting work in your field of expertise.

If you were not receiving your CPP pension, you would have to remit CPP premiums on your net self-employment earnings (your gross income—what you invoice to clients, less your business expenses).

When you're self-employed you don't have an employer (except yourself!), so you have to pay your own CPP premium plus a matching amount for your "employer." That's two times 4.95%, or 9.9%. That maximum in 2009 is double the Yearly Maximum Contributions for employees—two times $2,118.60, or $4,237.20.

So, by electing to receive your CPP pension early, and therefore cutting off the requirement to pay CPP premiums on future earnings, you'll save up to $4,237.20 per year. Now that's something worth thinking about!

This strategy works for self-employed people. Just make sure you don't work during the month before and the month during which you start to receive the CPP pension. That's what I'm going to do when I turn sixty—stop working for two months, elect to start receiving the CPP pension and then go back to work CPP premium-free.

MONEY-SAVING TIP: EMPLOYEES

A client of mine that is still working at age sixty-five told me that she took a leave of absence from her job for two months when she turned sixty. After the two-month hiatus and before she went back to work she applied to start receiving her CPP pension. The result? She started collecting CPP early as per the recommendation and she gets the added benefit of no more CPP deductions off her paycheque year-after-year from age sixty until she stops working.

Before you do this, communicate with your payroll department to make sure there are no adverse consequences to things like your pension plan. The last thing you need is something like a break in service to disrupt your hard-earned pension and other benefits.

WARNINGS

There is something important that seniors need to be aware of: the impact of one spouse dying. When one spouse dies it can have a significant effect on the total CPP pension amount that will be received by the surviving spouse.

When a CPP contributor dies, CPP pays three kinds of survivor benefits:

1. **The death benefit.** This is a one-time lump-sum payment (currently a maximum of $2,500).
2. **The children's benefit.** This monthly amount is paid to a dependent natural or adopted child of the deceased contributor, or a child in the care and control of the deceased contributor at the time of death. The child must be either under age eighteen, or between the ages of eighteen and twenty-five and in full-time attendance at a school or university.
3. **The survivor's benefit.** This is a monthly benefit for the spouse or common-law partner.

To qualify for any or all of these benefits, the deceased contributor must have contributed to the CPP for a minimum of three years.

If you are receiving your CPP retirement pension and your spouse or common-law partner dies, you need to apply for a survivor's benefit. In this case you will receive a combined monthly benefit.

Catch #1

The amount of a combined survivor's/retirement benefit is limited to the maximum retirement pension. For example, if you begin receiving a combined benefit in 2009, the most you will receive is $908.75 a month. In other words, if you have been eligible to receive the maximum CPP pension because you contributed to the plan during your working life, you won't receive anything extra on the death of your spouse or common-law partner. That hurts.

Catch #2

If the surviving spouse or common-law partner is age sixty-five or older and not receiving any CPP benefits of their own, they are eligible for a maximum of only 60% of the contributor's retirement pension. It should be noted that the rules in this area are exceedingly complex for people under sixty-five, people with disabilities, and situations involving dependent children.

Catch #3

There's also the shock of the surviving spouse losing the deceased spouse's OAS pension—a maximum of $516.96 a month or $6,203.52 per year in 2009.

For couples on a tight budget, these issues can lead to significant financial difficulties for the surviving spouse or common-law partner.

CONCLUSION

OK. There you have it. All you need to know about the CPP plan and how to optimize the amount you get out of it. Has your financial advisor discussed all this with you? He or she should have—it's a key part of your retirement strategy.

8

THE MONEY MAXIMIZER

Let's face it, we'd all like more money, right? Well, what's the best way to get it?

We could try to find another job that pays more. Perhaps we could work a lot more hours in our existing job in the hopes of getting a raise. If we are self-employed we could put in more hours at work in the hopes of making more profit.

Alternatively we could cut down our expenses by maybe forgoing a vacation this year or reducing our entertainment budget. Either way—increasing our income *or* reducing our expenses—it's likely to be a somewhat painful experience.

Would you be willing to spend a few hours looking at your financial big picture to see if there is something about your financial life that you could change to increase your cash flow? What if there was a spreadsheet that would allow you to calculate the total cash inflow over your entire life under many different scenarios so that you could choose the one that maximizes your family's cash inflows—without the pain of working more hours or reducing the expenses that make your life more enjoyable?

Well, there is such a spreadsheet. It's called the "Money Maximizer" and I'm going to show it to you in this chapter.

WHY WORK AGAINST THE TAXMAN?

When we talk about maximizing your money, we are actually talking about maximizing your after-tax cash inflows. For example, we have seen that if you make $80,000 in salary in 2009 in Ontario, you would owe $19,568.31 in federal and Ontario income taxes, $2,118.60 in CPP and $731.79 in EI premiums. Total deductions would therefore be $22,418.70 ($19,568.31 + $2,118.60 + $731.79), leaving you with only $57,581.30 in after-tax cash ($80,000 − $22,418.70). You make $80,000 but you can't spend all of it because you have to pay tax and other deductions first.

If there was a way to reduce your taxes by perhaps $3,000, you would be left with $60,581.30 in after-tax cash—an additional $3,000 that you can do with as you please. That's a lot easier than working harder to earn additional salary, since that additional salary requires you to work *much* harder and it's taxed. That's like trying to run a race carrying a fifty-pound sack of potatoes—the additional taxes weigh you down.

For example, in Ontario in 2009 you would have to increase your salary by $5,302, to $85,302, to be left with $60,581.30, the amount you were left with by reducing your taxes by $3,000. That's because in that tax bracket, an additional $5,302 in salary attracts $2,302 in federal and Ontario income taxes, leaving you with an additional $3,000 in after-tax cash.

THE VALUE OF TIME

There is another concept we have discussed previously that is key to maximizing your after-tax income: the time value of money. It's so important I'd like to review it again before we start.

Put simply, a dollar saved today is worth more than a dollar saved a year from now. That just makes sense. If you had a dollar today you could spend it, or invest it, or pay down debt with it. If you had to wait a year for that dollar, it would be worth less because you had to forgo the spending, couldn't invest it to earn a rate of return and couldn't pay down debt with it to reduce your interest expenses.

But how much less is that dollar worth? Well, it depends on something called the "discount rate." That's the interest rate that's in effect for the situation. For example, if you could invest that dollar in a GIC earning 5% a year, the discount rate to use is 5%. Using a discount rate of 5% on a dollar received a year from now yields a net present value (NPV) of $0.95. In other words, $0.95 invested today would be worth $1 a year from now because $0.95 times 1.05 is $1 (actually, $0.9975).

Don't worry if you don't really grasp the concept of discount rates and NPV calculations—you don't really need to. But you do need to buy into the concept because it is absolutely vital when you start talking about large dollar values over many years. Let's look at that now.

THE TIME VALUE OF MONEY

When we talk about retirement planning, the long term is basically your lifetime. For you it doesn't get any longer than that.

Say you are thirty years old and live to age ninety. That's sixty years of time you have to deal with. But what you do at age thirty is incredibly more significant than what you do at age eighty. In other words, if you can save $1,000 at age thirty, the benefit to you is much greater than if you saved $1,000 sixty years from now.

That's why in the following discussions, I will always mention the NPV affect of any change. It will effectively show the significance of a change in strategy, taking into account when it happens—the time value of money. For example, in the previous case, a change in strategy that saves us $1,000 this year is worth $1,000 in NPV. Saving $1,000 sixty years from now is only worth $53 today, when discounted at 5% a year.

THE MONEY MAXIMIZER SPREADSHEET

The Money Maximizer is a spreadsheet that will show you the after-tax cash inflow of you and your spouse or common-law partner from today to the end of your projected lifespans, taking into account federal and Ontario income taxes. It will show you the total after-tax cash inflows from today until the end of both your lives, as well as the NPV of those future cash flows.

As we saw in the chapter on income splitting, the key to reducing your family's income taxes is to focus on your as well as your spouse's or common-law partner's tax situation. That's why the spreadsheet has a column for you and your spouse or common-law partner—side-by-side—so that you can see the effect on your bottom line, your combined after-tax cash flows.

The real value of the spreadsheet is that it allows you change variables such as amounts, rates of return and time frames to see what the effect is on your after-tax cash inflows—the total as well as the NPV of your and your spouse's total cash inflows during your lifetimes.

It has the following worksheets or tabs at the bottom of the screen that you can click on to go to a separate section of the same spreadsheet:

- **Home.** This tells you a bit about the spreadsheet, including the version number and what it does.
- **Questions.** This is where you and your spouse or common-law partner answer all the questions needed to do the calculations.
- **Summary 30–95.** This is the summary screen showing all the information about each of your and your spouse's or common-law partner's income, taxes and after-tax cash inflows for as many as sixty-five years. It also shows the combined after-tax cash flows discounted to the present day—the NPV of all future after-tax cash flows.
- **Summary 30–95 You.** This shows your yearly OAS and CPP income amounts, RRIF minimum required withdrawals, RRIF extra withdrawals, any RRSP income, other income.(e.g., from self-employment after you retire) and any OAS benefits repayments (clawbacks).
- **Summary 30–95 Spouse.** This is the same as the previous tab, but for your spouse or common-law partner.
- **Summary Results.** This tab pulls the results from Summary 30–95 so you can summarize and compare various scenarios to determine the best way to maximize your after-tax cash flows.

- **Retirement Results You.** This tab shows the year-by-year income from your RRSP, OAS, CPP and RRIF withdrawals (minimum and additional to meet your cash flow needs) from as early as age fifty-five to age ninety-five. It also tracks your RRSP and RRIF values to show whether you'll run out of money while you still have need for it.
- **Retirement Results Spouse.** This is the same as the previous tab, but for your spouse or common-law partner.
- **Assumptions.** These are the assumptions that went into the spreadsheet.

The following is a screen shot of the Home screen of the Money Maximizer:

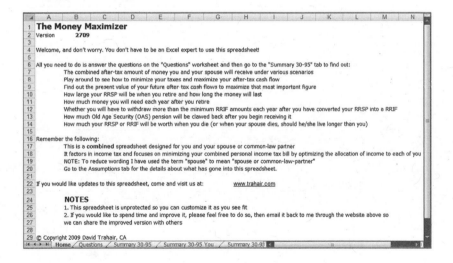

Note the tabs at the bottom. The Home tab is the active tab and is shown in bold.

MEET PAT AND JANE

In this chapter and throughout the remainder of this book I will be using an example of a married Canadian couple named Pat and Jane. In this case Pat is "You" and Jane is the "Spouse" (I have used "spouse" to mean "spouse or common-law partner" to save space in the spreadsheet). These individuals are fictitious and their situation will almost certainly not be the same as yours, but here's the good part: the spreadsheet is available to you free as a reader of this book. Simply go to http://www.trahair.com and click on the link to the cover of this book. The Excel spreadsheet then can be downloaded to your computer for your own use.

Here are all the details Pat and Jane punched into the "Questions" tab on the spreadsheet. Please bookmark this page, as future chapters will be investigating the financial effect of making changes to one or more of the answers that Pat and Jane have given here:

General

	Pat	Jane
What is today's date?	11/19/2009	11/19/2009
What is your last name?	Smith	Smith
What is your first name?	Pat	Jane
On what date were you born?	1/2/1978	1/2/1983
In what province/territory do you reside?	Ontario	Ontario
Would you like to split your pension income with your spouse?	N	N
Would you like to split your CPP pension income with your spouse?	N	N
What percent of your self-employment earnings (if any) could you split with your spouse?	0.00%	0.00%

RRSP/RRIF

What was the total market value of your RRSPs on the most recent statement?	$30,000	$0
How much do you plan to contribute to your RRSP each year from now until retirement?	$8,000	$0
At what age do you plan to retire and stop making RRSP contributions?	65	65
At what annual rate of return do you expect your RRSP investments to grow **until** you retire?	5.00%	5.00%
At what annual rate of return do you expect your RRSP or RRIF investments to grow **after** you retire?	4.00%	4.00%
What average annual rate of inflation do you expect over the remainder of your life?	2.00%	2.00%

Old Age Security

Are you eligible for the maximum Old Age Security (OAS) pension at age sixty-five? (Y=Yes, N=No) (If you have lived in Canada for at least forty years after turning eighteen, you will receive the maximum pension.)	Y	Y
If you haven't met the above condition, how many years will you have lived in Canada since your eighteenth birthday when you turn sixty-five? (You must have lived in Canada for at least ten years to qualify for OAS.)		

Canada Pension Plan

Are you eligible for the maximum Canada Pension Plan (CPP) pension at age sixty-five? (Y=Yes, N=No) (If on average from age eighteen to retirement your earnings exceeded the maximum pensionable earnings [$44,900 in 2008], you will receive the maximum CPP pension.)	Y	N
If not, what has your average annual income from earnings been since you turned eighteen? (Enter a figure between $5,000 and $44,900.)		$0
Would you like to start receiving your CPP pension between the ages of sixty and sixty-five? (It will be reduced by 6% for each year before age sixty-five.)	N	N
If so, at what age would you like to start receiving your CPP pension? (Enter an age between sixty and sixty-four.)		

Other Income

In today's dollars, how much money (before tax) from other sources do you expect each year after you retire? (Sources include a pension, self-employment, rental property, and investments outside your RRSP.)	$0	$0
At what age do you expect this income from other sources to stop?		

Spending

What is your current total income before taxes (i.e., salary or net income from self-employment)?	$90,000	$0
What percentage of your income before tax in today's dollars do you think you will need after you retire? (Note: The rule of thumb says about 70%, but depending on your situation it could be much lower—perhaps 40%.)	50%	50%

Longevity

Until what age do you think you will live? (Your answer must be seventy or older.)	82	82

Here is a screen shot of the top section of the "Questions" tab of the spreadsheet:

	A	B	C	D	E	F	G	H	I	J	K	L	M
1	**Money Maximizer Questions**												
2												Your	Spouse's
3	Answer these questions in column L for yourself and column N for your spouse:											Answers	Answers
4													
5	**GENERAL**												
6		What is today's date?										11/19/2009	11/19/2009
7		(e.g., 11/19/2009 or 19/11/2009)											
8													
9		What is your last name?										Smith	Smith
10													
11		What is your first name?										Pat	Jane
12													
13		On what day were you born?										1/2/1978	1/2/1983
14		(e.g., 1/13/1978 or 13/1/1978)											
15													
16		In what province/territory do you reside?										Ontario	Ontario
17													
18		Would you like to split your pension income with your spouse?										N	N
19													
20		Would you like to split your CPP pension income with your spouse?										N	N
21													
22		What percent of your self-employment earnings (if any) could you split with your spouse?										0.00%	0.00%
23													
24	**RRSP/RRIF**												
25		What was the total market value of your RRSPs on the most recent statement?										$30,000	$0
26													
27		How much do you plan to contribute to your RRSP each year from now until retirement?										$8,000	$0
28													
29		At what age do you plan to retire and stop making RRSP contributions?										65	65

Home Questions Summary 30-95 Summary 30-95 You Summary 30-9

A WORD ABOUT DATE FORMATS (MM/DD/YEAR VERSUS DD/MM/YEAR)

It always used to confuse me when typing dates as numbers—is it MM/DD/YEAR or DD/MM/YEAR. It's not confusing for days after the twelfth of the month, but for days one to twelve it is.

For example, is 1/6/2008 January 6, 2008 (MM/DD/YEAR) or June 1, 2008 (DD/MM/YEAR)? The answer seems to be that in Canada the accepted format is DD/MM/YEAR and in the U.S. it's MM/DD/YEAR. That confuses me because I find the MM/DD/YEAR format easier to understand. I am interested in knowing the month before the day since it's more important. It's also the order I would write it if I was using the word for the month, i.e., I would write "January 6, 2008" not "6 January, 2008."

That leaves me as a Canadian using the accepted U.S. format, but so be it. It's easy to set your computer so that your dates show up the way you like in the various programs you use (such as Microsoft Excel). To set it up in Microsoft Windows, go to the "Start" button, then select "Control Panel," then "Regional and Language Options." Here if you select "English (United States)" it will show the "short date" format as MM/DD/YEAR. Selecting "English (Canada)" will show it as DD/MM/YEAR.

Pat and Jane: The Assumptions

The beauty of a spreadsheet is that you can change any variable you wish to see what the effect is on after-tax cash flow. In this case I have made the following assumptions. Remember, you can make your own assumptions for your own situation:

- **Salary.** I have added an inflation factor to Pat's $90,000 salary by increasing it at the rate of inflation input above of 2% a year from this year (age thirty-one) until age sixty-five.
- **RRSP contributions.** I have kept the $8,000 RRSP contributions constant at $8,000 a year.
- **OAS and CPP pension income.** I have increased these amounts by the 2% inflation rate, as this is what the government does.
- **Income tax rates.** Income taxes are computed for all years at the 2008 Ontario rates.
- **RRSP and RRIF withdrawals.** These are assumed to take place on January 1 of each year.
- **Basic personal exemption and age amounts.** These have not been indexed to inflation.

A NOTE ABOUT PROJECTIONS

A projection like the one the Money Maximizer produces will never give an exact answer because the future has many unknowns. For example, tax rates and personal exemptions will most certainly change. RRSP limits and minimum RRIF withdrawals might change (in fact, the minimum RRIF withdrawal rates were reduced by 25% for 2008 in response to the economic crisis). There is also uncertainly about income—very few people will have full-time employment each and every year with a salary that rises by inflation.

The key point, however, is that the Money Maximizer does provide an excellent way to compare one situation to another. For example, say we want to compare earning a salary to earning a similar amount of self-employment income, allowing us to split income with our spouse. We assume the basic personal exemption stays at $9,600 for the next sixty years, which most certainly won't be the case. Because the basic personal exemption will change in future years, the spreadsheet won't give us a perfect figure for the after-tax cash inflows. But it will provide an accurate calculation of the *difference* between the two situations, and that's key to our decision making. Let's move on and you'll see what I mean.

Pat and Jane: The Results

The Money Maximizer projects that Pat and Jane's after-tax cash inflows from 2009 to 2065, the year of Jane's death, will total $5,131,822. That's a lot of dough.

But what about on a discounted basis, the more important figure because it takes into account the time value of money?

That total is $1,607,555, still a significant sum, but much less than $5 million. That's because in this case, as in your case, a lot of the cash flow is received many years from now and must be discounted to today's dollars so we can compare apples to apples.

Here's a screen shot of the top section of the "Results" tab of the spreadsheet:

	A	B	C	D	E	F	G	H	I	J
1	**Money Maximizer Summary Results**									
4				Tax	First Name	Pat	Jane	Pat	Jane	Pat
5				Form	Age	31	26	32	27	33
6				Line	Year	2009	2009	2010	2010	2011
7	Total income									
8	Employment income (box 14 T4 slip)		101	ENTER		90,000	0	91,800	0	93,636
9	Old Age Security pension (box 18 T4A(OAS) slip) (Age 65 and older)		113	COPY*						
10	CPP or QPP benefits (box 20 T4A(P) slip) (Age 60 and older)		114	COPY*						
11	CPP pension split (You to Spouse)			Auto		0	0	0	0	0
12	CPP pension split (Spouse to You)			Auto		0	0	0	0	0
13	Other pensions or superannuation		115	ENTER		0	0	0	0	0
14	Elected split-pension amount (Form T1032)		116	ENTER		0	0	0	0	0
15	RRIF minimum withdrawals (Age 72 and older)			COPY*						
16	RRIF extra withdrawals (Age 72 and older if needed)			COPY*						
17	RRIF value taxed on death			ENTER						
18	Taxable amount of eligible dividends			Blank						
19	Actual dividend x 1.45 (Public Companies)		120	ENTER						
20	Taxable amount of ineligible dividends			Blank						
21	Actual dividend x 1.25 (Small Businesses)		180	ENTER						
22	Interest and other investment income (Schedule 4)		121	ENTER						
23	Rental income (net)		126	ENTER						
24	Taxable capital gains (50% of actual net gains Schedule 3)		127	ENTER						
25	RRSP income (T4RSP slips) (Age 55 to 71)		129	COPY*						
26	Other income (CPP ineligible) (Age 55 and older)		130	ENTER						
27	Self-employment income (net)		135	ENTER		0	0	0	0	0
28	Self-employment transfer (You to Spouse)			Auto		0	0	0	0	0
29	Self-employment transfer (Spouse to You)			Auto		0	0	0	0	0
30	This is your total income		150	Auto		90,000	0	91,800	0	93,636
32	Net income									
33	Registered pension plan deduction (box 20 T4, box 32 T4A)		207	ENTER						
34	RRSP deduction (Schedule 7)		208	Auto		8,000	0	8,000	0	8,000
35	Deduction for elected split-pension amount (Form T1032)		210	Auto		0	0	0	0	0
36	Child care expenses (Form 778)		214	ENTER						
37	Carrying charges and interest expenses (Schedule 4)		221	ENTER						
38	Deduction for CPP contributions on self-employment		222	Auto		0	0	0	0	0
39	Total line 207 to 222		233			8,000	0	8,000	0	8,000
40	This is your net income before adjustments		234			82,000	0	83,800	0	85,636

Summary 30-95 / Summary 30-95 You / Summary 30-95 Spouse / Summ

And here is a screen shot of the same tab but further down, showing the total after-tax cash inflows on a non-discounted and discounted basis:

	A	B	C	D	E	F	G	H	I	J
1	**Money Maximizer Summary Results**									
4				Tax	First Name	Pat	Jane	Pat	Jane	Pat
5				Form	Age	31	26	32	27	33
6				Line	Year	2009	2009	2010	2010	2011
7	Total income									
48	Total Further deductions			Auto		0	0	0	0	0
50	This is your taxable income		260	Auto		82,000	0	83,800	0	85,636
52	Refund or Balance owing									
53	Net federal tax (Schedule 1 line 52)		420	Auto		12,190	0	12,658	0	13,136
54	CPP contributions payable of self-employment earnings (Schedule 8)		421	Auto		0	0	0	0	0
55	Social benefits repayment (OAS clawback line 235)		422	Auto		0	0	0	0	0
56	Provincial or territorial tax (Form 428)		428	Auto		6,527	0	6,841	0	7,160
57	This is your total payable		435			18,717	0	19,499	0	20,296
60	After-tax Cash Inflow Before CPP and EI			Auto		63,283	0	64,301	0	65,340
61	(Equals Net Income less Total Payable)									
63	TOTAL AFTER-TAX CASH INFLOW									
64	After-tax Cash Inflow Before CPP and EI					63,283	0	64,301	0	65,340
65	Less:									
66	CPP contributions through employment					-2,049	0	-2,049	0	-2,049
67	Employment insurance premiums					-711	0	-711	0	-711
69	TOTAL AFTER-TAX CASH INFLOW					60,522	0	61,541	0	62,580
72	Combined Annual After-tax Cash Inflow			Auto			60,522		61,541	
74	Total Combined After-tax Cash Inflows						5,131,822			
76	Net Present Value all Future After-tax Cash Inflows			Auto			1,607,555			
77	(at 5% per year)									
79	CALCULATION AREA BELOW THIS LINE									

Summary 30-95 / Summary 30-95 You / Summary 30-95 Spouse / Summ

Pat and Jane Try Income Splitting

Currently Pat earns a salary of $90,000 a year and Jane doesn't work. This puts Pat in a high tax bracket and does not take advantage of Jane being in the lowest bracket.

What do you think the dollar effect would be if Pat could split, or allocate, some of the income to Jane? Unfortunately, if Pat has a normal salaried job, the ability to split income is limited. But if Pat was a self-employed contract worker, things could change.

Let's say Pat earns self-employment earnings of $90,000 instead of salary, and then could pay a wage to Jane for services including bookkeeping, sales and marketing, and strategic planning for Pat's business. We'll assume a wage of $27,000 (30% of $90,000) is reasonable.

We'll also assume Pat's $90,000 self-employment income increases at the 2% inflation rate, as we did previously when it was salary.

All we need to do is change a couple of answers on the "Questions" tab in the spreadsheet. We change the answer to "What percent of your self-employment earnings (if any) could you split with your spouse?" to 30%.

You may also note another interesting effect: Jane now has earnings and must contribute to CPP. She will therefore be building up her CPP retirement nest egg and will be able to rely on that income from as early as age sixty.

We'll need to change Jane's answer to the question under the CPP heading because she is under the maximum pensionable earnings for CPP of $44,900 (for 2008). We input $27,000—the amount of income allocated from Pat for 2008.

Now we move to the "Summary 30–95" tab and move Pat's initial $90,000 salary from the tax form line 101 (Employment income) to line 135 (Self-employment income [net]) in the column for Pat in 2009 (age thirty-one).

The results? Total combined after-tax cash inflows are $5,502,777—$370,955 more than if Pat were salaried ($5,502,777 − $5,131,822). The NPV of the future after-tax cash flows is $1,672,710—ahead of the salaried scenario by $65,155 ($1,672,710 − $1,607,555).

The conclusion is not that Pat should simply become self-employed. That may be impossible given the circumstances. Maybe in Pat's line of work you need to be salaried, or maybe Pat can't stand the idea of being self-employed. That's not the point. The point is that the spreadsheet empowers you to play with "what if" scenarios to see what effect a decision might have on the big picture—your family's combined after-tax cash inflows.

Putting the RRSP "Start Late" Theory to the Test

Let's put the "start late" theory to the test with Pat and Jane. Pat has $30,000 in an RRSP and contributes $8,000 per year for thirty-five years (from age thirty-one to age sixty-five). I've assumed the RRSP grows by 5% per year.

At age sixty-five Pat's RRSP has built up to a value of $838,136 and provided sufficient income to Pat's expiration at age eighty-two. This scenario gives a total after-tax cash inflow figure of $5,502,777 and a NPV of after-tax cash flows of $1,672,710.

Let's assume Pat and Jane buy a house in 2018, when Pat is forty years old, for $333,333. They put a down payment of $83,333 from an inheritance and assume a mortgage of $250,000 for the remainder.

You can easily do a Google search on the Web for "Mortgage Calculator" to find websites that will calculate mortgage payments. I just punched in a $250,000 mortgage amount, at 6% a year over an amortization period of twenty-five years. The online calculator yielded a monthly payment of $1,599.52. That's $19,194.24 annually. Assuming the interest rate stays the same for the twenty-five years, this mortgage will be paid off in 2043 when Pat is sixty-five years old.

Let's look at doing things differently. Pat and Jane decide at thirty-one that they don't want to follow the "RRSP at all costs" route to retirement savings. They decide to forgo any RRSP contributions until the mortgage is paid off. Will they be able to build up an RRSP of $838,136 by Pat's sixty-fifth birthday? Let's see.

From now (2009) until 2018 when they buy the house, Pat does not make the $8,000 annual RRSP contribution. This is where the

Money Maximizer spreadsheet comes in handy. I simply changed Pat's RRSP contribution answer to $0 from $8,000. The tax bill for Pat in 2009 went to $22,190 from $18,717—an increase of $3,473. That means Pat has a marginal tax rate of 43.4%, including Ontario surtaxes. So Pat is left with an extra $4,527 in after-tax cash inflow during 2009 (the $8,000 that didn't go to an RRSP less the $3,473 in additional taxes). For nine years, from 2009 until 2017, Pat has an extra $4,527 to work with.

Let's assume Pat invests that money in a TFSA that allows a maximum of $5,000 a year. Because Pat has sworn off the stock market, the money is invested in 100% safe GICs returning 3% a year. The $4,527 a year, growing at 3% a year for nine years, would build to a value of $45,990.

Pat and Jane will then be able to put $129,323 down on their home purchase in 2018 (the $83,333 they have from an inheritance, plus the $45,990 in the TFSA). Their mortgage will then be $204,010 (the purchase price of $333,333 less $129,323 down).

Their monthly mortgage payments over twenty-five years will be only $1,305.27, not $1,599.52. But just a minute. Pat and Jane want to eliminate their mortgage ASAP. They want to increase their mortgage payments to pay it down faster. They decide to add the $4,527 a year to the payments. That's an additional $377.25 a month ($4,527/12 months). So instead of paying $1,599.52 a month, they pay $1,976.77 a month ($1,599.52 plus $377.25).

The mortgage will be paid off in twelve years, not twenty-five. That would leave Pat mortgage-free in 2030 at age fifty-two. For the next thirteen years, Pat makes RRSP contributions with the money that was going to the mortgage—$1,976.77 a month or $23,721.24 a year. Assuming Pat's marginal tax rate is still 43.4%, Pat will get a tax refund of $10,295.02 that first year that will also roll back into the RRSP, resulting in further tax refunds. The RRSP will only be invested in 100% safe GICs.

Pat's Tax Turbo-Charged RRSP

Let's get back to Pat's real, not theoretical, RRSP and assume it earns an average rate of return of 3.95%—the average rate of return from

1998 to 2008 on the laddered GIC strategy we calculated in Chapter 2. Here's what that would build to for Pat in thirteen years:

The Tax Turbo-Charged RRSP

Year	Pat's Age	RRSP Value January 1	RRSP Cash Contribution	Tax Refund Prior Year Contribution	Total RRSP Contribution	Growth in RRSP (3.95% a year)	RRSP Value at December 31
2030	52	$0	$23,721	$0	$23,721	$937	$24,658
2031	53	24,658	23,721	10,295	34,016	2,318	60,992
2032	54	60,992	23,721	14,763	38,484	3,929	103,405
2033	55	103,405	23,721	16,702	40,423	5,681	149,509
2034	56	149,509	23,721	17,544	41,265	7,536	198,309
2035	57	198,309	23,721	17,909	41,630	9,478	249,416
2036	58	249,416	23,721	18,067	41,788	11,503	302,707
2037	59	302,707	23,721	18,136	41,857	13,610	358,175
2038	60	358,175	23,721	18,166	41,887	15,802	415,864
2039	61	415,864	23,721	18,179	41,900	18,082	475,846
2040	62	475,846	23,721	18,185	41,906	20,451	538,203
2041	63	538,203	23,721	18,187	41,908	22,914	603,025
2042	64	603,025	23,721	18,188	41,909	25,475	670,409
2043	65	$670,409	$23,721	$18,189	$41,910	$28,137	$740,455

In 2030 Pat contributes $23,721 and the next year receives a tax refund of 43.4% of that—$10,295. The next year, Pat puts in the regular $23,721 but also adds the tax refund on the prior year's total contribution of $34,016. That's 43.4% of $34,016, or $14,763. The opening RRSP value plus the total contribution for the year grows at the annual rate of 3.95% for the next thirteen years.

As you can see, the "start late" strategy builds Pat's RRSP contributions to $740,455. But to this we must add the original $30,000 Pat has in 2009. That, projected to 2043 at a 3.95% annual return, will be worth $111,983. Pat's total RRSP will be worth $852,438, whereas the RRSP strategy from age thirty-one at 5% builds an RRSP of $838,136.

Pat would be further ahead by $14,302 with a Tax Turbo-Charged RRSP strategy using 100% safe, government-guaranteed GICs.

CONCLUSION

Now it's your turn. Go to http://www.trahair.com, click on the image of this book, and download the Money Maximizer for your own use. Then you can begin to make some real significant progress towards a worry-free retirement.

HOW TO RECOVER FROM THE STOCK MARKET CRASH

OK, you're close to retirement, maybe in your late fifties or early sixties, and used to be pretty well set for your golden years. You worked your butt off and made RRSP contributions even during those years when doing so was very difficult.

You listened to the experts and trusted the stock market. You may have been talked into things like income trusts that you now know are usually high-risk equities that don't guarantee cash flow.

Perhaps you even diversified geographically. Just like the experts recommended, you put money in the U.S. You put money in China. You also entered the emerging markets.

In a nutshell, you built a well-diversified portfolio of equities and fixed-income investments like government bonds.

And you still got clobbered.

Here's why. The following list from Bloomberg.com shows the returns of the major benchmark indexes for 2008, converted to Canadian dollars. Remember: this is the return for the whole year. The return from the peak reached during June to the end of the year would be worse.

- S&P/TSX Composite Index: −33.4%
- S&P 500 Index: −22.61%
- NASDAQ U.S. Stock: −26.28%

- MSCI European and Asian Stock Market: −30.08%
- Emerging Countries Stock: −42.87%

You may even have been unfortunate enough to have had money in companies that went bankrupt. Or perhaps with an investment advisor that could not be trusted.

The sad truth is that your retirement nest egg has been severely damaged.

Now what?

THE DEVASTATING EFFECT OF THE CRASH

Most mutual fund salespeople agree that you should reduce your exposure to equities (the stock market) as you grow older. The reason is simple: if you don't you could get killed financially.

Let's go back to the end of 2008. Say a seventy-year-old senior had 100% of his $200,000 portfolio invested in equity mutual funds that emulated the S&P/TSX Composite Index. As discussed earlier, during the period June to November of 2008, the index lost 45% of its value. That means his $200,000 retirement nest egg got scalped by $90,000—to only $110,000.

It's a tragedy. How in heaven's name is he going to earn that amount of money back? Trust the stock market again? I don't think so.

WARNING: I have actually seen the following recommendation in print.

I have even seen it recommended, in a book written by a well-known financial type, that you should take out a loan to invest in the stock market to make up for stock losses. Are you kidding me? You get decimated in the stock market, so you borrow money to try and make up for it? Give me a freakin' break.

ARE YOU GOING TO THROW GOOD MONEY AFTER BAD?

At this point you are probably a little freaked out about your retirement plans.

Unfortunately, there is no magic solution to solve the problem. But surely you aren't going to trust the "system" to make up for what it just took away, are you?

If 2008 taught us anything, it was that people nearing retirement should have reduced their exposure to equities. Well, now is not the time to increase your exposure to them in the hopes of winning your money back. As far as I'm concerned, that's throwing good money after bad. It's gambling. It's risking personal financial disaster.

Here's my advice: get out of equities altogether if you can.

Given that we aren't going to trust the stock market to make up for what it took away, what is there that you can do to make your retirement a happy one?

Here are my thoughts.

YOU CAN STILL RETIRE WELL

You can't change the past and you can't control what the stock market does. The key to retiring well is to forget about what you can't change or control and focus on what you can.

There are several vital factors that you still have control over, factors that with a little tweaking could add years to your retirement funding.

Let's bring back the Money Maximizer spreadsheet for Pat and Jane to see what the dollar value impact of each change is.

Throughout this chapter we'll use the basic situation described in the last chapter. Here's a summary of where we'll start:

- Pat is thirty-one and Jane is twenty-six in 2009.
- Pat has a job that pays $90,000 in salary in 2009 and that salary increases at 2% a year.
- Jane does not work and therefore makes no payments into the CPP plan.
- Pat works to age sixty-five in the year 2043.
- Pat's RRSP is worth $30,000 in 2009 and Pat makes RRSP contributions of $8,000 every year until retirement.
- Pat's RRSP grows at an average annual rate of return of 5% up to retirement and 4% thereafter.
- Inflation is assumed to be 2% per year.
- Pat and Jane are both eligible for the maximum OAS pension.
- Pat elects to start receiving the CPP pension at age sixty-five.

- Since Jane never works, she is not eligible for the CPP pension.
- Neither Pat nor Jane earn any other income after retirement (i.e., from self-employment or rental property, etc.).
- Pat and Jane estimate that they'll need 50% of Pat's pre-retirement income to maintain their standard of living after retirement.
- Pat and Jane live to age eighty-two.
- When Pat dies at age eighty-two in 2060, the balance in Pat's RRIF is transferred tax-free to Jane.
- Jane dies at age eighty-two in 2065.

The Money Maximizer shows that in 2009, Pat and Jane's after-tax cash inflows will total $5,131,822 and that on a discounted basis the total is $1,607,555.

Those figures are from today, when Pat is only thirty-one.

We want to do some figuring for when Pat and Jane are close to retiring, so let's ignore the years from 2009 to 2038. Pat is now sixty and Jane is fifty-five. That's where we want to be—close to retirement. What happened in the past is water under the bridge.

Under the scenario just described for Pat and Jane, according to the Money Maximizer spreadsheet the total of their after-tax cash inflows from 2038 until they both cease to exist is $2,663,050. On a discounted basis the present value (in 2038 dollars) is $1,674,037. Keep these figures handy, as we'll be comparing them to the totals that different strategies result in. I'll call this the "base scenario."

Note also that we'll build on the previous results. In other words, the most beneficial situation will be kept for the figures produced in the next section. For example, you'll see that CPP pension splitting makes sense in Pat and Jane's case. We'll assume they elect to split Pat's CPP pension income in making the next decision about whether to elect to receive the CPP early. Since you can use the Money Maximizer, you can decide to do it differently if you wish.

1. CPP Pension Splitting

As we have discussed, making sure you minimize your taxes through effective income splitting is paramount. This includes the CPP pension, RRIFs, annuitized RRSPs and any other pensions you may have.

Neither Pat nor Jane has a company pension plan, but only Pat has paid into the CPP. What is the dollar impact of electing to split Pat's CPP pension income?

The total after-tax cash inflows increase to $2,683,209 and $1,685,112 on a discounted basis. That's an improvement of $20,159 and $11,075, respectively.

2. Electing CPP Early

Here's one of those interesting conclusions that I did not expect. It shows the power of a spreadsheet in making decisions.

Remember the chapter on the CPP where we concluded that it makes sense to elect to receive the CPP as soon as you retire, because of the time value of money? I also then suggested that you may wish to take a leave of absence for a couple of months and then elect to start receiving CPP early. The benefit is that you'll then no longer have to make CPP contributions.

In this case, if Pat elects to start receiving CPP at age sixty, Pat no longer has to make CPP contributions from age sixty until retirement at age sixty-five.

The results? Total after-tax cash inflows are $2,668,137 and $1,714,285 on a discounted basis. That result is interesting. The total cash inflows are $15,072 higher than in Scenario 1, when Pat and Jane just split the CPP pension and waited until age sixty-five, but on a discounted basis, Pat and Jane are $29,173 further ahead.

It's interesting because Pat is further ahead by electing to receive the CPP pension early, even though Pat is in the highest tax bracket and will be paying a high rate of tax on the CPP pension income received from age sixty to sixty-five. For someone in a lower tax bracket, the benefit of electing the CPP early would be even more significant, as taxes on the income would be lower.

It also shows the benefit of no longer having to pay the CPP premiums.

3. RRSP/RRIF Income Splitting

Pat has built up an RRSP—not a spousal RRSP—so all the RRSP and RRIF income that is received goes on Pat's income tax return. As we have seen, however, the new pension income-splitting rules allow RRSP annuity income after age sixty-five and RRIF income to be split with a spouse or common-law partner.

Let's elect for Pat to split RRSP/RRIF income with Jane.

Pat and Jane's total after-tax cash inflows increase to $2,699,948 and $1,731,875 on a discounted basis. That's an improvement of $31,811 and $17,590, respectively, over Scenario 2.

4. Extending Your Retirement Date

One of the best ways to set yourself up for a solid retirement is to delay your retirement date a little bit.

Even staying in the workforce for one extra year can have a huge impact on the number of years your retirement nest egg will last, because you are bringing in money instead of draining it, while your investments benefit from another year of growth.

What happens if Pat works just one additional year and instead of retiring at age sixty-five, makes it sixty-six?

Pat and Jane's total after-tax cash inflows increase to $2,864,113 and $1,826,171 on a discounted basis. That's an improvement of $164,165 and $94,296, respectively. As you can see this has the most significant impact of any of the other changes we have seen.

Other Ideas

Spend less in retirement. In my experience, people tend to get more frugal as they age. This is a good thing for those who aren't that naturally frugal, but the real penny pinchers are liable to hold back too much during retirement. What good is sacrificing your life to die with $1 million in the bank? On the other hand, there is real potential for the penny pinchers to teach the spenders how to get more for less when they are on a fixed income.

Make money in retirement. Even earning in a few thousand dollars a year from a hobby or what you enjoy doing can bring a huge relief to the amount of money you'll need to stash away for retirement. Perhaps a rental property could provide a good cash flow. There are many creative ways to help fund your retirement.

CONCLUSION

The investment peddlers used to tell us "Just invest with me, and relax." Make a resolution not to believe them any longer. Don't throw any more good money after bad.

Retiring well is not going to be easy. But that's just the point—it never was.

10
THE ALTERNATIVES: CAN ANYTHING BEAT AN RRSP?

The simple truth about RRSPs is that for lower-income Canadians they don't make sense. First of all, they probably don't have any excess money after paying the bills to even make a contribution. Recommending that these people borrow to invest in an RRSP is simply irresponsible. Even if they have the money, the tax refund at a lower income bracket for many of these people will be pennies on the dollar. There are also other problems lurking, like the clawback of government low-income subsidies because of RRSP investment values.

A COMMON MISCONCEPTION
Before we delve into the details, let me clear up one common misconception: RRSPs do not equal equities. RRSPs are registered plans that can hold many different things including equities (stocks or mutual funds that invest in stocks), bonds and GICs. An RRSP is therefore not "risky" by definition. It is if all you decide to put in it is equities, but not if you simply buy GICs in it. Don't confuse RRSPs with the actual investment instruments that they may contain.

ALTERNATIVES TO RRSPs
Even if RRSPs make sense for a person, there are many alternatives: investing outside an RRSP, investing in real estate, investing in your

own business, the new Tax-Free Savings Accounts (TFSAs), and possibly forming a corporation and leaving profits in at the low rate of tax and drawing dividends out after retirement.

But are any of these alternatives better than an RRSP?

INVESTING OUTSIDE VERSUS INSIDE AN RRSP

The debate over whether to invest inside or outside an RRSP has been going on for many years. If I sold investments for a living, I'd probably feed you a line we often hear: get the best of both worlds by maximizing your RRSP contribution *and* investing outside your RRSP!

Well, I don't sell investments. I know how tough it is to make even partial RRSP contributions after paying for the house, the kids, food and all the rest. I also know that if you can't maximize your RRSP contribution it's not the end of the world.

In fact, you may know that there are billions of dollars in unused RRSP contribution room—the amount that people could have contributed to their RRSP but didn't. You know what? Forget about it. It's not the major problem it's made out to be. For most people, maximizing their RRSP at all costs, even if they have to borrow, is the last thing they should do. It could lead to lots of debt and, as we saw in 2008, plummeting RRSP values. If that isn't a recipe for personal financial disaster I don't know what is.

OK, enough said. But what do you do with the money you do have? To invest inside or outside an RRSP is the question. Here's my analysis of the issue.

We know that investing in RRSPs has two main benefits: the tax refund/deferral and the fact that the investments grow (hopefully!) on a tax-deferred basis. If all the stars align correctly, we will get a high tax break when we are working, our RRSP will grow and we will pay a lower rate of tax when we retire (since our income will be lower) and we will only have to pay it many years from now.

But there is one fly in the ointment. If we believe in the stock market and are using equities (stocks) in our RRSP, the capital gains when we sell the investments to take out retirement funds later are converted to income. In other words, in an RRSP you effectively pay tax on 100% of the gain between what you paid for the stock or mutual fund and what you sold it for.

This is not the case outside an RRSP, where you only pay tax on 50% of the capital gain (the 50% of the capital gain is called the "taxable capital gain").

Is the tax hit you take by holding equities in your RRSP enough to make investing outside an RRSP a better alternative?

Let's see. We'll use the following simple situation:

- original investment of $10,000 is made on January 1, 2009
- marginal tax rate of 46%
- annual growth rate of the investment is 6%
- investment growth compounds annually
- investment is cashed in after ten years, on December 31, 2018
- discount rate to factor in time value of money is 5%

We'll start with an RRSP and we'll assume the tax refund is received at the end of 2009, a year after the contribution was made.

It's vital that we factor in the value of the timing of the outflows and inflows. That shows the time value of money. Remember, $1 received today is worth more than $1 received a year from now.

Here are the results.

Invest in an RRSP	1/1/2009	12/31/2009	12/31/2018
Original investment (out) in	($10,000.00)		$17,908.48
Income tax refund (cost)		$4,600.00	($8,237.90)
Net after-tax (outflow) inflow	($10,000.00)	$4,600.00	$9,670.58

Present value at 5%	
Original investment	($10,000.00)
Tax refund	$4,380.95
Final after-tax amount	$5,936.90
Total net present value at 5%	$317.85

At a 46% marginal tax bracket, a $10,000 RRSP contribution will yield a $4,600 tax refund.

The original $10,000 grows to $17,908.48 after ten years. That's an annual growth rate of 6% a year. (Take a calculator and punch in 10,000, then multiply by 1.06, get the result and keep doing that nine more times and you should get $17,908.48.)

The tax on the withdrawal of $17,908.48 is 46% of the total (remember, there is no capital gains tax in an RRSP) and that's $8,237.90 of tax. The after-tax amount left is $9,670.58.

Here's the tricky part: we need to discount the $4,600 tax refund received a year from today and the $9,670.58 received ten years from now. Those present value figures are $4,380.95 and $5,936.90, respectively.

Add the outflows and inflows together and you'll find that the net present value of the outflows and inflows is $317.85 in today's dollars.

Now let's look at what would have happened if we invested the $10,000 in the same equities but outside an RRSP. Obviously there'd be no tax refund because there's no RRSP contribution, but how do the numbers shake out with the reduced tax on the capital gain? Here's that result.

The income tax cost is calculated as follows: proceeds of $17,908.48 less the adjusted cost base (ACB) of $10,000 equals a capital gain of

Invest Outside an RRSP—Equities	1/1/2009	12/31/2018
Original investment (out) in	($10,000.00)	$17,908.48
Income tax cost		($1,818.95)
Net after-tax (outflow) inflow	($10,000.00)	$16,089.53

Present value at 5%		
Original investment	($10,000.00)	
Final after-tax amount	$9,877.57	
Total net present value at 5%	($122.43)	

$7,908.48. The taxable capital gain is 50% of that, or $3,954.24. Tax at 46% of $3,954.24 is $1,818.95.

That will leave cash in hand of $16,089.53. Discount that amount to today's dollars and you get $9,877.57.

Add the outflows and inflows together and the net present value of the outflows and inflows is ($122.43)—a negative figure—in today's dollars. That's $440.28 lower than the RRSP value of positive $317.85.

If I change the investment period to twenty years, the RRSP comes out ahead by $734.01. After thirty years, the RRSP comes out ahead by $792.28.

We obviously must be aware that each situation is different. There is also the issue around RRSPs having to convert into RRIFs that have minimum withdrawal requirements, whereas investments outside an RRSP can be cashed with little or no restrictions. Tax rates may also be higher or lower than this example.

But the key here is that we're comparing apples to apples. It is the same investment whether inside or outside an RRSP. We are also using the same discount rate in each case. Given that you should do your own specific calculations, it appears the math indicates a pretty consistent answer: investing in equities in an RRSP usually beats investing outside because of the huge benefit of an immediate tax refund.

The RRSP wins.

INVESTING IN REAL ESTATE

I was at the movies last night and during the fifteen-minute sales pitch before the show there was an ad from a real estate company. It said in bold letters "The stock market has lost half its value. Invest in a sure thing: real estate."

Real estate is *not* a sure thing. The value of properties can, and often do, rise and fall just like the stock market.

You may be tempted to look at rental properties as a good investment. Rent it out and have the rental income cover the mortgage payments and operating costs, while the value of your investment increases. I have often thought that it may make sense for a real estate agent, who knows a particular area really well and could spot a bargain when it became available, to invest in a rental property rather than an RRSP.

It does make some logical sense. She would have an intimate knowledge of her investment and could keep an eye on it as she does her job.

But once again risk comes into play and in my opinion trumps the strategy. In this case, the real estate agent has the vast majority of her wealth in one thing: real estate. She has her home, her job and her rental property tied up in illiquid real estate investments. If the market tanks, what happens? Possible job loss, maybe an inability to rent out the rental property, and the pressure of trying to keep up the mortgage payments on a principal residence that may have lost value.

Once again, seems too risky to me. The RRSP wins again.

INVESTING IN YOUR OWN BUSINESS

I have been self-employed for over twenty years. It's sometimes not easy, but I love it. I would not go back to a full-time job for double what I make now. There are many people that are in a similar position and they know what I know: it takes money to run a small business. What about investing in yourself, in your own business, instead of RRSPs?

Well, you'd run into the same problem as in the real estate idea— what if your business fails? You've lost everything by putting all your eggs in the one basket. Once again, diversifying your wealth by investing in an RRSP makes sense here, too.

Just before we leave this subject, however, I'd like to make another observation. I encourage you to try self-employment. There is no such thing as a job-for-life anymore. Even pension plans can go bankrupt. Unfortunately you could get the axe any day.

Protect yourself. At least try self-employment on a part-time basis to see how it fits. You may need to find work at a later time to help pay the bills.

Your only protection is to educate yourself. Make yourself marketable by learning how to do what you love and make money doing it.

INVESTING IN
A TAX-FREE SAVINGS ACCOUNT

In 2008 the federal government introduced a product called the Tax-Free Savings Account (TFSA), which I've mentioned earlier in the book from time to time.

Is it a good alternative to an RRSP? Let's find out.

Beginning in January 2009, you can put up to $5,000 per year into this type of plan and the income (interest, dividends, capital gains, etc.) that is earned on the contributions is never taxed. The TFSA is available to any Canadian resident individual (other than trusts) eighteen years of age and older.

Main Features of the TFSA

- Generally you are allowed to invest in the same products that qualify for investments in your RRSP.
- Unused contribution room will be carried forward indefinitely.
- The CRA states that it will determine the contribution room for each individual who files a personal income tax return.
- Any withdrawals will be added to the contribution room for the following year.
- The contribution room will be indexed to inflation after 2009, rounded to the nearest $500.
- Interest on money borrowed to make a contribution is not deductible for tax purposes.
- Losses in a TFSA cannot be used to offset gains or income earned outside a TFSA.
- Upon death, there is a deemed disposition (it's treated like you cashed it in) just prior to the death, so accumulated income and capital gains that were earned up to the date of death are tax-exempt.
- The plan can be left to a surviving spouse and maintain its tax-exempt status, or can be transferred to the surviving spouse's plan without affecting the spouse's contribution room.
- Upon a marriage breakdown, transfers are allowed to the former spouse's plan and this will not increase the amount of contribution room of the transferor or reduce the contribution room of the transferee.
- For non-residents, existing plans will continue to be tax exempt, no contributions will be allowed while non-resident and no contribution room will accrue while non-resident.
- The TFSA can be used as collateral for a loan.
- There will be a 1% tax on excess contributions, similar to other registered plans.

This plan is especially important if you are conservative like me. In fact, in my opinion, as I have said many times before, when it comes to personal finances you should not risk the farm. That means staying out of the stock market.

We've already discussed how anyone who trusted the TSX with their house deposit money may have seen it drop by 30% or more in 2008. That's why it makes more sense to stick to the strategy—invest only in no-risk, no-fee, government-guaranteed investments like GICs, term deposits and high-income savings accounts.

When held in regular (non-RRSP, non-TFSA) investment accounts, however, the interest on our no-risk products are taxed each and every year at our marginal tax rate (the rate at which each additional dollar is taxed, given all your other income and deductions). That's one of the main benefits of the TFSA—no income tax on the earnings.

The other tax advantage is that the withdrawals from the TFSA are not included in income or used for federal income-tested benefits like the Canada Child Tax Benefit (CCTB), Employment Insurance (EI), the Goods and Services Tax Credit (GSTC), the Guaranteed Income Supplement (GIS), the Working Income Tax Benefit (WITB) or the clawback of Old Age Security (OAS).

The TFSA as an Income Splitter

Remember our friend income splitting to reduce our family tax bill? Well, the TFSA is ideal for anyone with kids eighteen years of age or older or a non-working spouse. That's because there is no "attribution" of income to you when you give funds to your family members to contribute to their TFSA.

In other words, if you give $5,000 to your spouse and he or she invests in a GIC outside a TFSA, the income (including any dividends) earned on that $5,000 must be reported on your, not his or her, income tax return. The income "attributes" back to you because it was your $5,000 to begin with. That's not the case with the TFSA. With a TFSA the interest earned would not be reported, period.

Opportunity for Retirees

Since there is no upper age limit for contributors, there is an opportunity for retired people that are no longer able to make RRSP contributions to reduce their taxes. For example, if you are over seventy-one and already drawing from your RRIF account, you could invest $5,000 in a TFSA to stop the taxation of the income on it.

Does Anyone Have $5,000 Outside a Registered Account?

In fact, anyone who already has $5,000 invested outside a registered account like an RRSP can transfer the investment to a TFSA and immediately stop the taxation of the income on the account. This is called a "transfer-in-kind."

This is ideal for fixed-income products like GICs, but you'll need to be careful with other investments like stocks and mutual funds. That's because you'll be deemed to have disposed of the investment at its Fair Market Value at the time of the transfer. Any inherent gains to that point will have to be reported on your tax return.

Here's the catch: Any capital losses will be deemed to be nil on a transfer of a losing stock or mutual fund to a TFSA. The solution to this is to sell the loser before the transfer and then put the $5,000 into the TFSA through a separate transaction.

Why the TFSA Is Better Than an RRSP for Home Buyers

The TFSA is a registered plan like an RRSP but is very different than an RRSP in that contributions to the TFSA are not tax-deductible. The flip side of this is that withdrawals from the TFSA are not taxable, and that includes any income earned in the plan.

This plan is ideal for saving for a house deposit, even better than an RRSP Home Buyers' Plan, for several reasons.

First of all, unlike an RRSP, you don't have to have "earned income" to create room for the contribution—everyone gets $5,000 per year starting at age eighteen. With an RRSP you need earned income (basically a salary or self-employment earnings) to create RRSP room. For example, say you are twenty-two and have just graduated from University in 2009. You make $20,000 during the rest of your graduating year. Your RRSP contribution room for the next year (2010) is $3,600 (18% of your prior year's earned income of $20,000).

With the TFSA, you'd be allowed to put $5,000 in for 2009 and another $5,000 for 2010 for a total of $10,000. Let's say you have your eye on a home that will cost $130,000 and that you'd like to put down a minimum deposit of 15% ($19,500). With the TFSA, you and your spouse would be able to do that by 2010. With an RRSP you'd have to wait for years until your earned income had totaled $108,333 to create $19,500 of RRSP room, since 18% of $108,333 is $19,500.

But there are more problems with an RRSP. First of all, when you are just starting out in the job market, your income is likely to be low. You are therefore in a low tax bracket and your RRSP contributions result in a low refund. For example, if your salary is between $15,327 and $36,020 in Ontario in 2008, your tax bracket was only 21.05%. In other words a $10,000 RRSP contribution would result in a $2,105 refund. Good, but not great.

The RRSP Home Buyers' Plan

Back in chapter 4, we discussed the RRSP Home Buyers' Plan (HBP), which allows first-time home buyers to withdraw up to $25,000 from their RRSP to purchase or build a qualifying home. This withdrawal is not taxed immediately and your RRSP issuer will not withhold tax on the amount, but there is a catch: The full amount must be repaid to your RRSP within fifteen years.

In other words, if you withdrew $20,000, $1,333 must be repaid to your RRSP each year for fifteen years or the required repayment amount ($1,333) is added to your taxable income so you'll have to pay income tax on it. This is the difficulty with the HBP. Once you have assumed responsibility for carrying a mortgage, you'll feel the pressure of making those mortgage payments, property taxes, repairs and main-tenance on your home, etc. You may find that coming up with $1,333 to replenish your RRSP each and every year may be difficult.

It would seem to me that you would be better off using a TFSA from the beginning to save for your home deposit.

If you are past this stage and have already invested in RRSPs and do not have savings outside your RRSP, using the HBP to invest in a home at the right time makes sense, since it's the only way you'll get that deposit and consequently your home.

KEEPING PROFITS IN A CORPORATION

If you have your own business that is run through a corporation, you may wish to consider using it as a tax deferral mechanism. Basically, the profits of an active business corporation are taxed in the company at a low rate of tax—less than 20%, in most cases. The low rate is meant to benefit small business owners by leaving more after-tax money in the corporation, enabling it to grow by investing in new equipment or hiring new people, for example.

You as the owner/shareholder are not taxed personally on corporate profits until you take the money out. If you take out all the profits as salary, you pay tax as a normal employee would, at whatever marginal tax rate you fall into. The salary expense to the corporation would then leave it with no profit to tax at the low rate. This effectively eliminates the advantage of the low corporate rate of income tax.

If, however, you don't need to take all the profits out, you can leave them in the corporation and pay tax at the low rate. Then, years later when you retire, you can withdraw the profits as dividends at a reduced personal tax rate. This is similar to what an RRSP does.

Once again this strategy runs the risk of putting all your eggs in one basket. The business could suffer some lean years or even go under. There are also issues related to the taxation of the investment income in the corporation not being active income subject to the low rate of tax. But if structured correctly, it may be something worth considering.

CONCLUSION

The alternatives to a simple RRSP have one major problem: it's hard to beat the tax deferral that an RRSP provides, especially for higher-income people.

And there are other problems with ignoring RRSPs. With alternative strategies like putting all your money in real estate, there is the problem of a lack of diversification. A downturn in the housing market when your home and your job, as well as your rental property, all depend on the housing market remaining solid is simply too risky.

The same can be said for investing in your own business.

Remember point number one of this book: avoid personal financial disasters. Putting all your eggs in one basket like real estate or self-employment puts you in a situation with the potential for personal financial disaster. Don't do it.

In fact, why even consider alternatives to an RRSP when you can use one to diversify your wealth, and it allows you to invest in 100% safe GICS that will never decline and are guaranteed by the federal government (through CDIC) even if the financial institution that issues them goes under?

Combine those benefits with the Tax Turbo-Charged RRSP strategy that allows you to start late and use the significant tax benefit of making RRSP contributions during your peak earnings years, and you've got a winning strategy.

11

THE ANTIDOTE SUMMARY

OK, you've hung in there for the whole book. Here's a summary of The Antidote. Follow it and you can rest easy, knowing that your retirement nest egg will never decline even if your bank goes under.

1. AVOID PERSONAL FINANCIAL DISASTERS
- Never touch anything that cannot be explained simply to you in plain English.
- Don't invest in anything that is not guaranteed by the government.
- Never borrow to invest.
- Avoid complicated investment schemes. If it sounds too good to be true, it is.

2. YOU DON'T NEED THE STOCK MARKET OR MUTUAL FUNDS
- The truth is that you don't need to risk your hard-earned money in the stock market and you don't need mutual funds.
- You can use 100% government-guaranteed investment certificates to achieve your goals without the risk of losing your shirt.
- If you want to take a chance, buy a lottery ticket.

3. BUY A HOME AND PAY OFF THE MORTGAGE

- Decide if you can afford a house and if you can, buy one.
- Do the calculation of how many years it will take to pay the mortgage off and do it.
- Never risk your home for any kind of investment idea, no matter what.

4. REDUCING EXPENSES DOESN'T HAVE TO BE PAINFUL

- Focus on two of your biggest expenses: income taxes and interest on your debt.
- Pay to have your family's personal income tax returns prepared by a qualified expert.
- Pay extra to have that expert analyze your family situation to maximize savings by income splitting, restructuring to make sure as much debt as possible is tax deductible.
- Find out what your credit rating is and improve it.
- Get at least three quotes on any debt that you get into.

5. FORGET RRSPs UNTIL YOUR DEBT IS PAID OFF (THE OPPORTUNITY ZONE)

- Do not even think about saving for retirement until you have paid off student loans and bought a home.
- Pay off the mortgage before investing another dime in an RRSP.
- Never borrow to invest in an RRSP.

6. ASK YOURSELF IF YOU REALLY NEED AN INVESTMENT ADVISOR

- If you've got a bad one, find a good one.
- If you can't find a good one, simplify your finances so you don't need one at all.

INDEX

INDEX

I

ICICI Bank Canada, 65
"illiquid securities," 38
iMac, 34
income, 89–90, 152
income splitting, 10
    annuity payments, RRSP,
      89, 90
    and combined tax, 91
    CPP Pension, 136–137
    and death of spouse, 89
    deferred profit sharing plan
      (DPSP), 90
    and employer-sponsored benefits,
      contributions, 89
    Life Income Funds (LIFs), 90
    and Money Maximizer, 157–158
    non-refundable tax credits, 92–93
    and OAS benefits, 91
    and registered pension plan (RPP),
      89
    RRIF withdrawals, 90
    survivor pension annuity, 89
    and tax advantage, 91
    and unused tax credits,
      91–92
income tax
    as expense, 10
    rates, and Money Maximizer, 155
    reducing, 147–151
income trusts, 163
"incremental cost of borrowing," 140
Individual Retirement Account (IRA),
    90
inflation, 55–56, 130, 140
ING Direct, 65
Institute of Chartered Accountants of
    Ontario (ICAO), 116
insurance companies, 63

interest
    on debt, 83–88
    as expense, 10
    payments, and GIC, 53
    rate, defined, 140
    rate, reducing, 87–88
    rate, risk, 37
    reducing, as an expense, 83–88
international reply coupons (IRCs),
    14
investment advisor
    advantages, 113–114
    assessing, 118
    choosing, 117–118
    commission, 45
    and fraud, 24
    need for, 11, 184
investment amount, GIC, 53
investment banks, 30–31
investment grade securities, 38
iPhone, 34
iPod, 34

J

Jane, and Money Maximizer, 151–161
Jimmy, 85–86, 87–88
job security, 103
Joe, 79–82
joint election, 90–91
Joint Election to Split Pension
    Income, 91
joint names, and CDIC, 51
judgments, and credit report, 76

K

keeping up with the Joneses, 29
Kyle, 136–137

INDEX